SOURDOUGH DISCARD

Recipes Cookbook

ZERO WASTE EDITION

The Busy Mom's Guide to Crafting the Most Delicious, Nutritious Delights with All-Natural Ingredients

EMMA BROOKS

EMBRACING ZERO WASTE 🌱

In our effort to make this cookbook as environmentally friendly as possible, we've chosen to exclude images. By reducing the resources needed for printing and shipping, we aim to minimize our carbon footprint and help you embrace a zero-waste lifestyle.

This decision aligns with our values of sustainability and responsible living. We hope that, through these recipes, you'll find inspiration to create beautiful, delicious meals while caring for our planet. Thank you for joining us on this journey towards a greener, more sustainable future.

SCAN THE QR CODE TO JOIN THE SOURDOUGH SISTERHOOD FACEBOOK GROUP!

CONTENTS OVERVIEW

STEP INTO THE WORLD OF SOURDOUGH

Welcome to the cozy world of sourdough baking, where every discard can be transformed into something wonderful. I'm Emma Brooks, a mom who understands the daily juggle of family life, work, and the desire to serve up wholesome, delicious meals without feeling guilty about wasting ingredients. If you've ever hesitated to throw away sourdough discard, or felt the pinch of rising grocery costs, this book is for you. We're going to turn those leftover bits into nutritious delights that not only nourish your family but also help you save money and reduce waste.

In this journey, you'll discover that creating healthy, homemade food can be both easy and deeply satisfying. We'll explore a range of simple, straightforward recipes designed for busy schedules, so you can whip up something special without spending hours in the kitchen. Think of this book as your friendly companion, offering tips and tricks to make the most of your sourdough discard, all while ensuring you're feeding your family with the best.

I know the importance of healthy eating, especially in a world full of processed foods. Here, you'll find recipes that are packed with nutrition and flavor, using natural ingredients that are both good for you and the planet. Let's embark on this delicious adventure together, transforming waste into wonderful, and making every meal a moment of joy and health for you and your loved ones.

As we dive into these recipes, remember that baking is not just about the end product, but the journey itself. Each step is an opportunity to create, to learn, and to share with those we care about. So, let's get started on crafting meals that are as delightful as they are nourishing, and make every discard a treasure in your kitchen. Welcome to a new way of baking that's as rewarding for the heart as it is for the home.

Emma Brooks

UNLOCK YOUR FREE STARTER GUIDE & 2 SPECIAL BONUSES

Welcome to your journey into the world of sourdough! As you dive into the pages of this cookbook, you'll discover how versatile and rewarding it is to bake with sourdough discard. But, to truly master the art of sourdough, you need a solid foundation, and that starts with a great sourdough starter.

I'm excited to offer you the most complete guide to creating and maintaining your sourdough starter, absolutely free. This guide is packed with step-by-step instructions, tips, and troubleshooting advice to help you keep your starter vibrant and your bread delicious.

To access this invaluable resource, simply scan the QR code below and embark on your path to becoming a sourdough expert.

By the way, by scanning the QR code you will also get access to 2 extra bonus guides:
1. Seasonal Swaps: Savvy Substitutions for Every Season
2. Sourdough Solutions: Swift Fixes for Sourdough Struggles

SOURDOUGH DISCARDS?

Now that you know how to start your sourdough starter, we can talk about discards.

Sourdough discard is the portion of a sourdough starter that you remove during the feeding process. A sourdough starter is essentially a mixture of flour and water that has been colonized by wild yeast and beneficial bacteria. This living mixture needs regular feedings of fresh flour and water to stay active and healthy. During these feedings, some of the starter is removed to make room for new flour and water, and this removed portion is what we call sourdough discard.

Unlike what its name might suggest, sourdough discard is far from being waste. It's a versatile ingredient that can be used in a variety of recipes, imparting a unique tangy flavor and a hint of that complex sourdough essence to whatever you create.

The Formation of Sourdough Discards
To understand how sourdough discard is formed, we need to look at the life cycle of a sourdough starter. When you first create a starter, you combine equal parts flour and water, which allows wild yeast and bacteria from the environment and the flour itself to start the fermentation process. Over time, these microorganisms consume the sugars in the flour, producing carbon dioxide gas, alcohol, and various acids that contribute to the sourdough's characteristic flavor and leavening power.

As the starter ferments, it becomes more acidic, and the population of yeast and bacteria continues to grow. To keep the starter balanced and to prevent it from becoming overly acidic or depleting its food supply, you regularly discard a portion and add fresh flour and water. This practice not only maintains the health and vitality of the starter but also prevents it from growing too large and becoming unmanageable.

Each time you feed your starter, you essentially refresh it with new nutrients, allowing the yeast and bacteria to thrive. The removed portion, or discard, contains the same active microorganisms, albeit in a less concentrated form since it hasn't been freshly fed. It's this leftover portion that you can collect and use in various recipes, ensuring nothing goes to waste.

Why Save Sourdough Discards?
The idea of saving sourdough discard might seem like an extra step, but it's a valuable one. Sourdough discard is incredibly versatile and can be used in everything from pancakes and waffles to cookies and muffins. It adds a depth of flavor and a delightful tanginess that elevates even the simplest dishes. Moreover, by using your discard, you're practicing a

form of kitchen sustainability, making the most out of every bit of your ingredients and reducing food waste.

The practice of utilizing sourdough discard also connects you to a long tradition of resourceful cooking. For centuries, bakers have found creative ways to use every part of their ingredients, and sourdough discard recipes are a continuation of that legacy.

STORING SOURDOUGH DISCARDS

Proper storage is key to maintaining its quality and making the most of your ingredients. Here's a detailed guide on how to store your sourdough discard effectively, ensuring it's ready to use whenever you need it.

The Go-To Method
The simplest and most convenient way to store sourdough discard is to keep it in the refrigerator. Place your discard in a clean, airtight container and store it in the fridge. This slows down fermentation and preserves the discard's tangy flavor and usability for up to a week. If you bake regularly, you can keep adding new discard on top of the old one, maintaining a single, manageable container. Be mindful of the discard's age and use the oldest discard first to prevent spoilage and ensure freshness.

Long-Term Storage
If you're not planning to use your discard within a week, freezing is an excellent option. Portion the discard into small amounts, such as tablespoons or cup measurements, and place them in silicone molds or ice cube trays. Once frozen, transfer the portions to a resealable freezer bag or container. Frozen discard can last for several months and is easy to thaw at room temperature for 12 hours before use. This method is perfect for those times when you want to bake without worrying about discard spoilage.

Room Temperature Storage
For short-term storage, you can keep sourdough discard at room temperature for up to a day. Use a jar with a loose lid to allow some airflow while preventing contamination. This method is handy if you plan to use the discard within the next 24 hours. Always inspect the discard for signs of spoilage, such as an off smell or visible mold, before using it.

Maintaining Freshness
To keep your discard fresh and ready for various recipes, avoid allowing it to accumulate for too long without use. Regularly incorporate discard into your baking routine to ensure you always have a fresh batch. If you notice any liquid separation, known as hooch, simply stir it back into the discard or pour it off if it's excessive.

Combining Discards
If you maintain multiple sourdough starters, you can combine discards from different batches. This practice is perfectly fine and can add complexity to your recipes, though it's essential to keep track of the combined discard's age and condition.

BREAKFAST & BRUNCH

APPLE CINNAMON MUFFINS

Preparation time: 20 minutes
Cooking time: 25 minutes
Servings: 4

INGREDIENTS:
- 1.5 cups sourdough starter discard
- 1 large apple, peeled and diced
- 1/2 cup granulated sugar
- 1/3 cup vegetable oil
- 1/2 cup whole milk
- 1 large egg
- 1 teaspoons vanilla extract
- 1.5 cups all-purpose flour
- 1 teaspoon baking soda
- 1/2 teaspoon ground cinnamon
- 1/4 teaspoon salt
- For topping: 2 tablespoons granulated sugar mixed with 1/2 teaspoon ground cinnamon

INSTRUCTIONS:
1. Preheat your oven to 375 degrees Fahrenheit and line a muffin tin with paper liners.
2. In a large mixing bowl, combine the sourdough discard, diced apple, sugar, vegetable oil, milk, egg, and vanilla extract. Stir until well combined.
3. In another bowl, whisk together the flour, baking soda, ground cinnamon, and salt.
4. Gradually add the dry ingredients to the wet ingredients, stirring just until combined. Avoid over-mixing.
5. Divide the batter evenly among the prepared muffin cups, filling each one about two-thirds of the way full.
6. Sprinkle the cinnamon sugar topping evenly over the batter in each muffin cup.
7. Bake for 25 minutes, or until the muffins are golden brown and a toothpick inserted into the center comes out clean.
8. Let the muffins cool in the tin for 5 minutes, then transfer to a wire rack to cool completely.

BAGELS

Preparation time: 90 minutes
Cooking time: 20 minutes
Servings: 4

INGREDIENTS:
- 1 cup of unfed sourdough discard
- 3 cups of bread flour
- 1 tablespoon of sugar
- 1.5 teaspoons of salt
- 1.5 teaspoons of instant yeast
- 1 teaspoon of baking soda
- 1/2 cup of warm water
- 2 tablespoons of honey (for boiling)
- Coarse salt or sesame seeds for topping (optional)

INSTRUCTIONS:
1. Begin by combining the sourdough discard, bread flour, sugar, salt, and yeast in a large mixing bowl. Stir them until everything is fully combined.

2. Slowly add in the warm water while mixing to form a stiff dough.
3. Once the dough has formed, knead it on a lightly floured surface for 5 to 7 minutes, or until the mixture is smooth and elastic.
4. Divide the dough into 4 equal pieces, shape each one into a ball, then gently press your thumb through the center to create a bagel shape.
5. Rest the formed bagels on the floured surface covered with a clean towel for about 30 minutes, or until they puff up slightly.
6. Meanwhile, preheat the oven to 425°F and bring a large pot of water to a boil. Add in the honey and baking soda, then reduce the heat to a simmer.
7. Boil the bagels one at a time for 1 minute on each side, then take them out using a slotted spoon and place them on a baking tray lined with parchment paper.
8. Sprinkle the bagels with coarse salt or sesame seeds, if desired.
9. Bake in the preheated oven for 20-25 minutes, or until the bagels are golden brown.
10. Remove the bagels from the oven and let them cool on a wire rack before serving.

BAGEL BOMBS

Preparation time: 90 minutes
Cooking time: 20 minutes
Servings: 4

INGREDIENTS:
For the bagels:
- 3 1/2 cups all-purpose flour
- 1 cup sourdough discard
- 1 1/2 cups warm water
- 1 tbsp sugar
- 2 tsp kosher salt
- 2 tsp active dry yeast

For the filling:
- 8 oz cream cheese, at room temperature
- 1/4 cup finely chopped fresh chives

For the topping:
- 1 egg (for egg wash)
- 2 tbsp Everything Bagel Seasoning

INSTRUCTIONS:
1. In a large bowl, combine the flour, sourdough discard, water, sugar, salt, and yeast. Mix until the dough begins to come together.
2. Knead the dough on a floured surface for about 10 minutes or until it becomes smooth and elastic.
3. Place the dough in a greased bowl, cover with a towel, and let it rise in a warm place for about 1 hour or until it doubles in size.
4. Preheat your oven to 425°F and line a baking sheet with parchment paper.
5. Roll out the dough onto a floured surface and divide it into 8 equal pieces.

6. Flatten each piece into a circle and place a spoonful of cream cheese and a sprinkling of chives in the center of each.
7. Gather the edges of the dough up and around the filling, pinching to seal it well.
8. Place the filled dough ball seam-side down on your prepared baking sheet. Repeat this process with the remaining dough and filling.
9. Brush each bagel bomb with the beaten egg and sprinkle them with Everything Bagel Seasoning.
10. Bake in the preheated oven for 20-25 minutes or until they're golden brown.
11. Remove from the oven and let the bagel bombs cool on the baking sheet for 5-10 minutes before serving. Enjoy your homemade sourdough discard bagel bombs!

BANANA BREAD

Preparation time: 20 minutes
Cooking time: 70 minutes
Servings: 4

INGREDIENTS:
- 1.5 cups of mashed overripe bananas (~4 medium bananas)
- 1 cup of sourdough discard, unfed or fed
- 1/4 cup of unsalted butter, melted
- 1/4 cup of vegetable oil
- 1 cup of granulated sugar
- 1/2 cup of brown sugar, packed
- 2 large eggs
- 1 teaspoon of vanilla extract
- 1.5 cups of all-purpose flour
- 1/4 teaspoon of salt
- 1.5 teaspoon of baking soda

INSTRUCTIONS:
1. Preheat your oven to 350°F (175°C) and grease a 9x5 inch loaf pan.
2. In a large bowl, mash the bananas until smooth. Add in the sourdough discard, melted butter, vegetable oil, granulated sugar, brown sugar, eggs, and vanilla extract. Stir until well combined.
3. In a separate bowl, mix together the all-purpose flour, salt, and baking soda.
4. Gradually add the dry ingredients to the banana-sourdough mixture, mixing just until the flour is incorporated.
5. Pour the batter into the prepared loaf pan, spreading it out evenly.
6. Bake for about 70-75 minutes, or until a toothpick inserted into the center of the loaf comes out clean. If the bread is browning too much but the center is still raw, cover with aluminum foil for the remaining cooking time.
7. Allow the banana bread to cool in the pan for about 10 minutes before transferring to a wire rack to cool completely.

BREAKFAST BURRITOS

Preparation time: 10 minutes
Cooking time: 20 minutes
Servings: 4

INGREDIENTS:
- 8 large eggs
- 1 cup Sourdough discard
- 4 flour tortillas (8 inch)
- 1 cup shredded cheddar cheese
- Salt and Pepper to taste
- 2 tablespoons unsalted butter
- Optional toppings: salsa, avocado, sour cream

INSTRUCTIONS:
1. Start off by beating the eggs in a large bowl until they're fully combined. Stir in the sourdough discard and season with salt and pepper according to your preference.
2. Heat a large non-stick skillet over medium heat. Once the skillet is hot, add the butter and allow it to melt.
3. Pour in the egg and sourdough mixture. Allow it to cook undisturbed for 1-2 minutes until it starts to set around the edges.
4. Using a spatula, gently stir the eggs from the edge towards the center, letting any uncooked egg flow underneath. Continue cooking, stirring occasionally, until the eggs are mostly cooked but still slightly runny.
5. Sprinkle shredded cheese evenly over the eggs. Reduce the heat to low and cover the pan. Let it sit for a few minutes until the cheese is melted and the eggs are fully cooked.
6. Meanwhile, warm your tortillas in a dry skillet over medium heat for just a few seconds on each side to make them pliable.
7. Spoon one-fourth of the cheesy egg mixture onto the center of each tortilla.
8. Fold the sides of the tortilla in toward the center and then roll up from the bottom to make a tight wrap.
9. Serve the breakfast burritos warm with your choices of salsa, avocado, or sour cream on top.

BREAKFAST CASSEROLE

Preparation time: 15 minutes
Cooking time: 45 minutes
Servings: 4

INGREDIENTS:
- 1 cup sourdough discard
- 5 large eggs
- 1/4 cup milk
- 1 cup shredded cheddar cheese
- 1/2 bell pepper, diced
- 1/2 onion, diced
- 1 medium tomato, diced
- 3/4 cup sliced mushrooms
- 1/2 tsp salt
- 1/4 tsp ground black pepper
- 2 tsp olive oil
- 1/2 cup cooked bacon bits or cooked sausage (optional)

INSTRUCTIONS:
1. Preheat your oven to 350°F (175°C) and lightly grease a 9x9 inch baking dish.
2. In a large bowl, whisk together the eggs, milk, salt, and pepper until well combined.
3. Stir in the sourdough discard until everything is well mixed.
4. Heat up a frying pan with 2 tsp of olive oil over medium heat. Once hot, add the diced onion and bell pepper to the pan, sautéing until softened.
5. Add in the sliced mushrooms and continue cooking until the vegetables are well cooked and the mushrooms have reduced in size.
6. Spread the sautéed vegetables evenly across the bottom of the greased baking dish. Then layer the diced tomatoes on top.
7. Pour the egg and sourdough mixture over the vegetables in the baking dish, ensuring that it covers everything evenly.
8. Sprinkle the shredded cheddar cheese on top of everything, and if you're using bacon or sausage, sprinkle that on as well.
9. Bake in the preheated oven for 40-45 minutes, or until the top is golden and the eggs are set.
10. Allow the casserole to cool for a few minutes before cutting into it. Then, enjoy your Sourdough Discard Breakfast Casserole!

BREAKFAST COOKIES

Preparation Time: 20 Minutes
Cooking Time: 15 Minutes
Servings: 4

INGREDIENTS:
- 1 cup of sourdough discard
- 1 1/2 cups of all-purpose flour
- 1/2 cup of granulated sugar
- 1/2 cup of brown sugar, packed
- 1/2 cup of unsalted butter, at room temperature
- 1 large egg
- 1 teaspoon of vanilla extract
- 1/2 teaspoon of baking soda
- 1/2 teaspoon of salt
- 1 cup of rolled oats
- 1/2 cup of dried cranberries or raisins
- 1/2 cup of chopped nuts, such as walnuts or pecans

INSTRUCTIONS:
1. Preheat the oven to 350°F (180°C). Line a baking sheet with parchment paper or a silicone baking mat.
2. In a large bowl, cream together the butter, granulated sugar, and brown sugar until light and fluffy.
3. Beat in the egg and vanilla extract until well combined. Stir in the sourdough discard.
4. In a separate bowl, whisk together the flour, baking soda, and salt. Gradually add this to the wet ingredients and mix until just combined.
5. Fold in the rolled oats, dried cranberries, and chopped nuts.
6. Drop tablespoons of dough onto the prepared baking sheet, spacing them about 2 inches apart.

7. Bake for 12-15 minutes, or until the edges are golden and the tops are set.
8. Let the cookies cool on the baking sheet for a few minutes before transferring them to a wire rack to cool completely. Enjoy them as a breakfast treat or anytime snack.

CEREAL BARS

Preparation time: 20 minutes
Cooking time: 30 minutes
Servings: 4

INGREDIENTS:
- 1 cup sourdough discard
- 2 cups rolled oats
- 1 cup mixed nuts and seeds (such as sunflower seeds, pumpkin seeds, almonds, and walnuts)
- 1/2 cup honey or maple syrup
- 1/2 cup dried fruits (such as raisins, cranberries, apricots)
- 1 teaspoon vanilla extract
- 1/2 teaspoon cinnamon
- Pinch of salt

INSTRUCTIONS:
1. Preheat your oven to 350°F (175°C) and line a baking pan with parchment paper.
2. In a large bowl, combine the sourdough discard, oats, mixed nuts and seeds, honey or maple syrup, dried fruits, vanilla extract, cinnamon, and a pinch of salt. Mix well until everything is fully incorporated.
3. Pour the mixture into your prepared baking pan, pressing down firmly to ensure it is evenly spread out.
4. Bake in the preheated oven for around 30 minutes, or until the edges are golden brown.
5. Remove from the oven and let it cool completely in the pan.

6. Once cooled, lift the parchment paper to remove the bar from the pan and place it on a cutting board. Using a sharp knife, cut the bar into even pieces.
7. Your sourdough discard cereal bars are now ready to be enjoyed. Store any leftovers in an airtight container.

CINNAMON ROLLS

Preparation time: 90 minutes
Cooking time: 25 minutes
Servings: 4

INGREDIENTS:
For the dough:
- 1 cup sourdough discard
- 1 cup whole milk
- 1/4 cup unsalted butter
- 3 1/2 cups all-purpose flour, plus extra for dusting
- 1/4 cup white sugar
- 1 teaspoon salt
- 1 packet (0.25 oz) active dry yeast

For the filling:
- 1/2 cup unsalted butter, at room temperature
- 1 cup light brown sugar
- 2 tablespoons ground cinnamon

For the frosting:
- 4 ounces cream cheese, at room temperature
- 1/4 cup unsalted butter, at room temperature
- 2 cups powdered sugar
- 1/2 teaspoon vanilla extract

INSTRUCTIONS:

1. Warm the milk in a small saucepan until it bubbles, then remove from heat. Mix in the butter; stir until melted. Let cool until lukewarm.
2. In a large mixing bowl, combine the milk mixture with the sourdough discard, sugar, salt, and yeast. Gradually add in the flour.
3. Dust a clean surface with flour and knead the dough for about 10 minutes until it is smooth and elastic. Place the dough in a greased bowl, cover with a clean tea towel and let rise in a warm place for 1 hour, or until dough has doubled in size.
4. In a small bowl, combine the softened butter, brown sugar, and cinnamon to form the filling.
5. Once the dough has risen, turn it out onto a floured surface and roll out to a rectangle. Spread the filling evenly over the dough.
6. Roll up the dough and slice it into 8 pieces. Place the pieces in a greased baking dish.
7. Preheat your oven to 375 degrees F (190 degrees C). While the oven is heating, let the rolls rise for about 30 minutes.
8. Bake in the preheated oven for about 25 minutes, or until the tops are golden brown.
9. While the rolls are baking, you can start on the frosting. Beat together the cream cheese and butter until smooth. Add the powdered sugar and vanilla and beat until smooth and fluffy.
10. Once the rolls have cooled down a bit, spread the cream cheese frosting on top. Serve them warm and enjoy!

CORNBREAD

Preparation time: 15 minutes
Cooking time: 20 minutes
Servings: 4 people

INGREDIENTS:

- 1 cup sourdough starter discard
- 1 cup all-purpose flour
- 1 cup yellow cornmeal
- 1/4 cup granulated sugar
- 1 teaspoon baking soda
- 1/2 teaspoon salt
- 1/2 cup whole milk
- 1/2 cup unsalted butter, melted
- 2 large eggs

INSTRUCTIONS:

1. Preheat your oven to 375°F (190°C) and lightly grease an 8-inch square baking dish.
2. In a large bowl, combine the all-purpose flour, cornmeal, sugar, baking soda, and salt. Stir until well combined.
3. In a separate bowl, mix together the sourdough starter discard, whole milk, melted butter, and eggs. Ensure that all ingredients are well combined.
4. Gradually add the dry ingredients into the wet ingredients. Stir until

the two are fully incorporated but be careful not to overmix.

5. Pour the cornbread mixture into your prepared baking dish, spreading evenly with a spatula.

6. Bake in the preheated oven for 20-25 minutes, or until the top is golden brown and a toothpick inserted into the middle comes out clean.

7. Let the cornbread cool in the dish for at least 10 minutes before slicing and serving. Enjoy your moist, slightly sweet, tangy Sourdough Discard Cornbread!

CREPES

Preparation time: 20 minutes
Cooking time: 30 minutes
Servings: 4

INGREDIENTS:
- 1 cup of sourdough starter discard
- 3 large eggs
- 1 cup of whole milk
- A pinch of salt
- 2 tablespoons of granulated sugar (use only for sweet crepes, skip for savory)
- 2 tablespoons of unsalted butter, melted and slightly cooled
- 1 teaspoon of vanilla extract (use only for sweet crepes, skip for savory)
- Additional butter for the pan

INSTRUCTIONS:

1. In a medium bowl, whisk together the sourdough discard and eggs until well combined.

2. Gradually whisk in the milk, followed by the salt. If making sweet crepes, also whisk in the sugar and vanilla extract.

3. Next, whisk in the melted butter, making sure to add it slowly to avoid cooking the eggs.

4. Let the batter rest for about 15 minutes. This allows the sourdough starter to hydrate fully and the gluten to relax.

5. Heat a small non-stick pan over medium heat. Add a little butter to coat the bottom of the pan.

6. Pour in about 1/4 cup of batter, tilting the pan in a circular motion so the batter coats the bottom evenly.

7. Cook the crepe for about 2 minutes, until the bottom is lightly browned. Flip it over and cook the other side for about 30 seconds.

8. Repeat with the remaining batter, adding a little more butter to the pan as needed.

9. Serve the crepes warm with your choice of sweet or savory fillings.

DUTCH BABY

Preparation Time: 10 Minutes
Cooking Time: 20 Minutes
Servings: 4

INGREDIENTS:
- 3 large eggs, room temperature

- 3/4 cup whole milk, room temperature
- 3/4 cup all-purpose flour
- 1/2 cup sourdough starter discard
- 1 tablespoon granulated sugar
- 1/4 teaspoons fine sea salt
- 2 tablespoons unsalted butter
- Confectioners' sugar for dusting
- Fresh fruits or syrup for serving

INSTRUCTIONS:

1. Preheat your oven to 425 degrees F (220 degrees C). Place a 10-inch cast iron skillet or oven-safe frying pan in the oven while it preheats.
2. In a blender, combine the eggs, milk, flour, sourdough discard, granulated sugar, and salt. Blend until the batter is smooth and frothy, this should take about 1 minute.
3. Carefully remove the hot skillet from the oven using oven mitts. Add the butter to the skillet and swirl it around until it completely melts and coats the bottom of the skillet.
4. Immediately pour the batter into the hot, buttered skillet. Return the skillet to the oven and bake for 20 minutes. The Dutch Baby should puff up and turn golden brown.
5. Remove the skillet from the oven (remember it's hot!) and let it cool for a few minutes. The Dutch Baby will deflate a bit, that's expected.
6. Dust the Dutch Baby with confectioners' sugar and top with your choice of fresh fruits or syrup.
7. Slice into four portions and serve immediately.

FRENCH TOAST

Preparation time: 15 minutes
Cooking time: 20 minutes
Servings: 4 people

INGREDIENTS:

- 1 cup Sourdough Discard
- 4 large Eggs
- 1 cup Whole milk
- 1 tsp Pure Vanilla Extract
- 3 tbsp Granulated Sugar
- 1/2 tsp Ground cinnamon
- 1/4 tsp Salt
- 8 slices Thick-cut bread (Brioche, Challah or a sturdy, rustic bread works well)
- Unsalted Butter, for cooking
- Syrup, Powdered Sugar, Fresh Berries and/or Whipped Cream for serving

INSTRUCTIONS:

1. In a large bowl, whisk together the sourdough discard, eggs, milk, vanilla extract, sugar, cinnamon, and salt until fully combined.
2. Place the bread slices into the mixture and let soak for about 30 seconds on each side. Make sure the sourdough mixture covers all parts of the bread.

3. Heat a large skillet or griddle over medium heat and add a small pat of butter, enough to lightly coat the surface.
4. Once the butter is melted and skillet is hot, add the soaked bread slices.
5. Cook until golden brown, about 2-3 minutes on each side. Make sure to watch carefully to prevent them from burning.
6. Serve the prepared Sourdough Discard French Toast hot with your favorite toppings like syrup, powdered sugar, fresh berries, or whipped cream.

FRITTATA

Preparation time: 15 minutes
Cooking time: 30 minutes
Servings: 4

INGREDIENTS:
- 6 eggs
- 1/2 cup sourdough discard
- 1 cup freshly grated cheddar cheese
- 1/2 cup diced bell peppers (any color)
- 1/2 cup chopped green onions
- 1/2 cup diced tomatoes
- Salt and pepper to taste
- 2 tablespoons olive oil

INSTRUCTIONS:
1. Preheat your oven to 350°F (175°C).
2. In a large bowl, whisk together the eggs, sourdough discard, cheddar cheese, salt, and pepper.
3. Heat the olive oil in an oven-safe skillet over medium heat. Add the bell peppers and green onions, sauté these until they are soft, which should take around 5 minutes.
4. Pour the egg mixture into skillet with vegetables and cook for about 5 minutes until edges start to pull away from the skillet.
5. Sprinkle the diced tomatoes on top of egg mixture.
6. Then place the skillet in preheated oven, bake for about 15-20 minutes, just until the eggs are set in the middle.
7. Remove from oven, let it cool for a few minutes and then slice the frittata into 4 pieces.
8. Serve warm and enjoy your Sourdough Discard Frittata!

GRANOLA BARS

Preparation time: 30 minutes
Cooking time: 30 minutes
Servings: 4

INGREDIENTS:
- 1 cup sourdough discard
- 4 cups old fashioned oats
- 1/2 cup honey
- 1/2 cup light brown sugar
- 1/4 cup butter, melted
- 1 tsp vanilla extract
- 1/2 tsp salt
- 1 cup mixed nuts (walnuts, almonds, and pecans), chopped

- 1/2 cup mixed dried fruits (cranberries, raisins, apricot), chopped
- 1/2 teaspoon cinnamon

INSTRUCTIONS:

1. Preheat your oven to 350°F, and line a 9x9 inch baking pan with parchment paper.
2. In a large bowl, mix together the sourdough discard, oats, honey, brown sugar, melted butter, vanilla extract, and salt until well combined.
3. Fold in the chopped nuts, dried fruits, and cinnamon.
4. Pour the mixture into the prepared baking pan, pressing down firmly to even out the surface.
5. Bake in the preheated oven for about 25 to 30 minutes, or until the edges are golden brown.
6. Let the bars cool completely in the pan on a wire rack before cutting into squares or rectangles.
7. Serve as a hearty breakfast or as a snack on the go.

LEMON POPPY SEED BREAD

Preparation time: 15 minutes
Cooking time: 45 minutes
Servings: 4

INGREDIENTS:

- 1 cup sourdough discard or starter
- 2 lemons, zest, and juice
- 3 tablespoons poppy seeds
- 1 cup granulated sugar
- 1/2 cup unsalted butter, room temperature
- 2 large eggs
- 1/3 cup milk
- 1 teaspoon vanilla extract
- 2 cups all-purpose flour
- 1/2 teaspoon salt
- 1 teaspoon baking powder
- 1/2 teaspoon baking soda
- Glaze: 1/2 cup powdered sugar mixed with 1-2 tablespoons lemon juice

INSTRUCTIONS:

1. Preheat your oven to 350°F (175°C) and grease a 9x5-inch loaf pan.
2. In a large bowl, combine the sourdough discard, lemon zest, lemon juice, and poppy seeds. Set aside.
3. In a separate bowl, cream together granulated sugar and butter until light and fluffy. Beat in eggs, one at a time, until well incorporated.
4. Mix in sourdough mixture, milk, and vanilla extract.
5. In another bowl, whisk together flour, salt, baking powder, and baking soda. Gradually add the dry ingredients to the wet ingredients, mixing just until combined.
6. Pour the batter into prepared loaf pan. Bake for 45-50 minutes, or until a toothpick inserted into the

center of the loaf comes out clean.

7. While the loaf is baking, prepare the glaze by whisking together powdered sugar and lemon juice. Adjust the consistency with extra juice or sugar to taste.
8. Allow the loaf to cool in the pan for about 10 minutes, then remove from pan and place on a wire rack.
9. While still warm, drizzle the glaze over the loaf. Allow to cool completely before slicing and serving.

MORNING GLORY MUFFINS

Preparation time: 20 minutes
Cooking time: 20 minutes
Servings: 4

INGREDIENTS:
- 1 1/2 cups all-purpose flour
- 1/2 cup granulated sugar
- 1/2 cup packed brown sugar
- 2 teaspoons baking soda
- 1 teaspoon ground cinnamon
- 1/2 teaspoon salt
- 2 eggs
- 2/3 cup vegetable oil
- 1/2 cup sourdough discard
- 1 teaspoon vanilla extract
- 1 apple, peeled and shredded
- 1/2 cup crushed pineapple, drained
- 2/3 cup shredded carrots
- 1/2 cup raisins
- 1/2 cup chopped walnuts

INSTRUCTIONS:
1. Preheat your oven to 350°F (175°C) and line a muffin tin with paper liners.
2. In a large bowl, whisk together the flour, sugars, baking soda, cinnamon, and salt.
3. In a separate bowl, combine the eggs, oil, sourdough discard, and vanilla extract. Mix until well combined.
4. Add the wet ingredients to the dry ingredients. Stir until just combined.
5. Next, fold in the shredded apple, crushed pineapple, shredded carrots, raisins, and chopped walnuts. Do not overmix.
6. Evenly divide the batter among the muffin cups, filling each about 2/3 full.
7. Bake for 20-25 minutes or until the muffins are golden brown and a toothpick inserted into the center comes out clean.
8. Allow the muffins to cool in the tin for 5 minutes before transferring to a wire rack to cool completely.

PANCAKES

Preparation time: 15 minutes
Cooking time: 20 minutes
Servings: 4

INGREDIENTS:
- 1 cup of sourdough discard/starter
- 1 cup all-purpose flour

- 2 large eggs
- 3/4 cup whole milk
- 2 tablespoons granulated sugar
- 1 teaspoon baking powder
- 1/2 teaspoon baking soda
- 1/4 teaspoon salt
- 1/2 teaspoon vanilla extract
- Butter, for cooking
- Maple syrup, for serving

INSTRUCTIONS:

1. In a large bowl, combine sourdough discard/starter, all-purpose flour, eggs, milk, sugar, baking powder, baking soda, salt, and vanilla extract. Stir until the mixture is well combined, but don't overmix.
2. Preheat a non-stick pan or griddle over medium heat and lightly grease it with butter.
3. Pour 1/4 cup of batter onto the pan for each pancake. Wait until bubbles form on the top and the edges look set, usually about 1-2 minutes, then flip the pancakes and cook for another 1-2 minutes until they're golden brown and cooked through.
4. Repeat with the remaining batter, adding more butter to the pan as needed.
5. Transfer the pancakes to a serving dish and keep them warm. Continue with the rest of the batter until it's all used up.
6. Serve the warm pancakes with a pat of butter and a good drizzle of maple syrup. Enjoy your hearty and tangy Sourdough Discard Pancakes!

POP-TARTS

Preparation time: 1 hour 20 minutes (includes resting time)
Cooking time: 20 minutes
Servings: 4

INGREDIENTS:

- 1.5 cups of all-purpose flour
- 1/2 cup sourdough starter discard
- 1/4 cup granulated sugar
- 1/4 cup unsalted butter, chilled and diced
- 1/4 teaspoon salt
- 2-3 tablespoons cold water
- 1/2 cup of your favorite flavor jam
- 1 large egg for egg wash
- 1 cup powdered sugar
- 2-3 tablespoons milk

INSTRUCTIONS:

1. In a mixing bowl, combine the flour, sourdough discard, sugar, and salt. Mix until it's well combined.
2. Add the chilled, diced butter to the dry mixture. Use your hands to work the butter into the flour until the mixture resembles coarse crumbs.
3. Gradually add cold water, one tablespoon at a time, until the dough just comes together. You may not need all the water.
4. Wrap the dough in plastic and refrigerate for at least 1 hour, or overnight for best results.

5. On a lightly floured surface, roll out the dough into a rough rectangle, about 1/8 inch thick.
6. Cut into rectangles that are 3x4 inches. Re-roll the scraps and cut again until you have 16 total rectangles.
7. Place 8 of the rectangles on a lined baking sheet. Spoon 1 tablespoon of jam onto each rectangle, leaving a small border around the edges.
8. Use a fork to crimp the edges of each pop-tarts, sealing the fillings inside.
9. Beat the egg in a bowl and brush over the top of each pop-tart.
10. Preheat your oven to 375°F (190°C).
11. Bake for about 20 minutes, or until the pop-tarts are golden brown.
12. While the pop-tarts are baking, make the glaze: whisk together the powdered sugar and milk until smooth.
13. Let the pop-tarts cool before drizzling with glaze.

SPINACH QUICHE

Preparation time: 20 minutes
Cooking time: 35 minutes
Servings: 4

INGREDIENTS:
- 1 cup of sourdough starter discard
- 2 cups of fresh spinach
- 4 large eggs
- 1 cup of grated cheddar cheese
- 1/2 cup of heavy cream
- 1/2 teaspoon of salt
- 1/4 teaspoon of black pepper
- 2 tablespoons of olive oil
- 1/2 onion, finely chopped

INSTRUCTIONS:
1. Preheat your oven to 375°F (190°C).
2. In a large skillet, heat the olive oil over medium heat. Add the onion to the skillet and sauté until it becomes translucent. This should take around 5 minutes.
3. Add the fresh spinach to the skillet and continue to sauté until the spinach wilts. This should take approximately 2-3 minutes. Remove from heat and let it cool.
4. In a large bowl, mix together the eggs, heavy cream, grated cheddar cheese, salt, and black pepper until well combined.
5. Stir in the sourdough discard into the egg mixture and mix gently until it is evenly incorporated in the mixture.
6. Add the cooled spinach and onions to the mixture and stir until well combined.
7. Pour the mixture into a greased 9-inch pie dish.
8. Bake in the preheated oven for about 35 minutes, or until the quiche is set and lightly browned on top.
9. Remove from the oven and allow it to cool for a few minutes before slicing and serving.

WAFFLES

Preparation time: 15 minutes
Cooking time: 20 minutes
Servings: 4

INGREDIENTS:
- 1 cup of Sourdough Starter Discard
- 1 cup of All-Purpose Flour
- 2 tablespoons of Granulated Sugar
- 1 teaspoon of Baking Powder
- 1/2 teaspoon of Baking Soda
- 1/2 teaspoon of Salt
- 2 Large Eggs
- 1/4 cup of Unsalted Butter (melted)
- 3/4 cup of Milk
- 1 teaspoon of Vanilla Extract

INSTRUCTIONS:
1. In a large mixing bowl, combine the sourdough starter discard, all-purpose flour, granulated sugar, baking powder, baking soda, and salt.
2. In a separate bowl, beat the eggs and then add the melted butter, milk, and vanilla extract.
3. Pour the wet ingredients into the dry ingredients, mixing just until everything is blended. Be careful not to over mix; a few lumps are fine.
4. Let the batter sit for about 5 minutes while you preheat your waffle iron. Once the iron is hot, pour in enough batter to fill the molds without overflowing.
5. Cook the waffles according to your waffle iron's instructions, usually 3-5 minutes or until the waffles are golden brown and crisp on the outside.
6. Remove the waffles from the iron and keep them warm while you repeat the process with the remaining batter.
7. Serve hot with your favorite toppings like syrup, fresh fruit, or whipped cream.

ZUCCHINI BREAD

Preparation time: 20 minutes
Cooking time: 60 minutes
Servings: 4

INGREDIENTS:
- 2 cups of all-purpose flour
- 1 cup of sourdough discard
- 1 1/2 cups of shredded zucchini (about 1 medium zucchini)
- 1 cup of granulated sugar
- 1/2 cup of brown sugar
- 1/2 cup of vegetable oil
- 2 large eggs
- 1 teaspoon of vanilla extract
- 1 teaspoon of baking soda
- 1/2 teaspoon of baking powder
- 1/2 teaspoon of salt
- 1/2 teaspoon of cinnamon
- 1/4 teaspoon of nutmeg

INSTRUCTIONS:
1. Preheat your oven to 350 degrees Fahrenheit. Grease and flour a 9x5-inch loaf pan.

2. In a large bowl, combine the all-purpose flour, baking soda, baking powder, salt, cinnamon, and nutmeg. Set aside.

3. In a separate bowl, combine the granulated sugar, brown sugar, vegetable oil, eggs, and vanilla extract. Stir in the sourdough discard until well mixed.

4. Gradually add the dry ingredients into the wet mixture, stirring until just combined.

5. Fold in the shredded zucchini until evenly distributed throughout the batter.

6. Pour the batter into the prepared loaf pan.

7. Bake in the preheated oven for 60 minutes, or until a toothpick inserted into the center comes out clean.

8. Remove the bread from the oven and let it cool in the pan for 10 minutes. Then, transfer the bread to a wire rack to cool completely.

9. Slice and serve your Sourdough Discard Zucchini Bread.

BREAD & ROLLS

ANADAMA BREAD

Preparation time: 150 minutes
Cooking time: 30 minutes
Servings: 4

INGREDIENTS:
- 1 cup sourdough discard
- 1/2 cup cornmeal
- 1 1/2 cups water
- 3 tablespoons unsalted butter
- 1/4 cup molasses
- 1 teaspoon salt
- 3 1/2 cups all-purpose flour
- 1/4 cup nonfat dry milk
- 2 1/4 teaspoons active dry yeast

INSTRUCTIONS:
1. In a small saucepan, combine cornmeal and water, bring to a boil. Cook for about 1 minute, or until the mixture thickens. Remove from heat.
2. Stir in the butter, molasses, and salt to the cornmeal mixture. Set aside and let cool to room temperature.
3. Once cooled, add the sourdough discard to the cornmeal mixture.
4. In a large mixing bowl, combine the all-purpose flour, nonfat dry milk, and active dry yeast. Add the cooled cornmeal mixture. Stir until well combined.
5. Knead the mixture on a flour-dusted surface for about 10 minutes, or until smooth and elastic.
6. Transfer dough to a greased bowl, cover with a towel, and let rise in a warm place for one to two hours, or until doubled in size.
7. Preheat your oven to 375°F (190°C) and grease a loaf pan.
8. Punch down the dough and shape it into a loaf. Place the loaf in the greased pan.
9. Bake for about 30 minutes in the preheated oven, or until the bread has a golden-brown crust and sounds hollow when tapped on the bottom.
10. Remove from oven and let cool for about 10 minutes before removing from the pan. Enjoy the Sourdough Discard Anadama Bread while it's still warm.

BAGUETTE CLASSIC FRENCH BREAD

Preparation time: 15 minutes
1st rise time: 2-3 hours
2nd rise time: 1-2 hours
Cooking time: 25 minutes
Servings: 4

INGREDIENTS:
- 2 cups of bread flour
- 1 cup of sourdough discard
- 1 teaspoon of salt
- 1 teaspoon of sugar
- 1/2 teaspoon of instant yeast
- 1 cup of warm water (temperature around 110°F)

INSTRUCTIONS:

1. In a large mixing bowl, combine the bread flour, salt, sugar, and yeast. Stir until mixed.
2. Add in the sourdough discard and warm water. This should bring the dough together. If it's still too dry, add a little more water.
3. On a lightly floured surface, knead the dough for about 10 minutes, until it becomes smooth and elastic.
4. Place the dough back into the mixing bowl and cover it with a clean, damp cloth. Let it rise at room temperature for about 2-3 hours, or until it doubles in size.
5. After the first rise, divide the dough into 4 separate pieces. Shape each piece into a baguette by rolling it into a long, thin cylinder.
6. Place each piece on a baking sheet lined with parchment paper. Cover again with a damp cloth and let rise for another 1-2 hours.
7. Preheat your oven to 450°F (232°C). Place a pan with water on the bottom rack of the oven. This will help to create steam and give the baguettes a crispy crust.
8. Using a sharp knife, make several diagonal slashes on the top of each loaf. This helps the bread to expand while baking.
9. Bake for 25 minutes, or until the baguettes are golden brown and sound hollow when tapped on the bottom.

10. Let them cool on a wire rack.

BREADSTICKS

Preparation time: 90 minutes
Cooking time: 15 minutes
Servings: 4

INGREDIENTS:
- 1.5 cups of all-purpose flour
- 1/2 cup of active sourdough discard
- 1 teaspoon of salt
- 1 teaspoon of granulated sugar
- 1/2 cup of warm water
- 2 tablespoons of olive oil
- 2 teaspoons of instant yeast
- 3 tablespoons of melted butter
- 1/2 teaspoon of garlic powder
- 1 tablespoon of fresh chopped parsley

INSTRUCTIONS:
1. Start by combining the warm water, sugar, and yeast in a large mixing bowl. Let it sit for 5 minutes until the yeast starts to foam.
2. Next, add in the sourdough discard and 1 tablespoon of olive oil to the yeast mixture. Stir until it's well combined.
3. Gradually start mixing in the flour and salt until a dough forms. If the dough is too sticky, you can add a little more flour until it's manageable.
4. Cover the bowl with a damp cloth and place it in a warm place for

about an hour, or until the dough has doubled in size.

5. Preheat your oven to 425°F (220°C) and line a baking sheet with parchment paper.
6. Once the dough has risen, moved it from the bowl onto a lightly floured surface and divide it into 8 equal parts.
7. Roll each piece of dough into a rope shape that is about 8 inches long and place them onto the prepared baking sheet.
8. Brush the remaining tablespoon of olive oil over each breadstick and sprinkle with garlic powder and chopped parsley.
9. Bake in the preheated oven for about 15 minutes, or until the breadsticks are golden brown.
10. Serve warm and enjoy your Sourdough Discard Breadsticks.

BRIOCHE

Preparation time: 120 minutes
Cooking time: 30 minutes
Servings: 4

INGREDIENTS:
- 1 cup of active sourdough discard
- 3 1/2 cups of all-purpose flour
- 1 tablespoon of instant yeast
- 1/4 cup of granulated sugar
- 2 teaspoons of salt
- 4 large eggs
- 1 cup of unsalted butter, softened and cubed
- 1 egg for egg wash
- Sesame seeds (optional)

INSTRUCTIONS:

1. In a large mixing bowl or that of a stand mixer, combine the sourdough discard, flour, yeast, sugar, salt, and eggs.
2. Mix on low speed until the dough comes together, which will take 5-7 minutes.
3. Gradually add the unsalted butter, continuing to mix on low until it is fully incorporated.
4. Increase to medium speed and knead the dough for another 10-15 minutes until it is smooth and elastic.
5. Cover the bowl and allow the dough to rise in a warm place for around 1.5 to 2 hours, or until it is almost doubled in size.
6. Punch down the dough and divide it into four equal parts. Roll each piece into a ball shape and place them in a greased 9x5 inch loaf pan. Cover the pan and allow it to rise for another hour.
7. Preheat your oven to 375°F (190°C).
8. Beat the remaining egg and gently brush the top of the risen dough. Sprinkle with sesame seeds if desired.
9. Bake for 30 minutes, or until the top is golden brown, and a temperature probe reads 190°F when inserted into the center of the loaf.
10. Remove your sourdough discard brioche from the oven and let it cool in the pan for 10 minutes.

Then turn it out onto a wire rack to cool completely before slicing and serving.

CHEDDAR BISCUITS

Preparation time: 15 minutes
Cooking time: 20 minutes
Servings: 4

INGREDIENTS:
- 1 cup of Sourdough Starter Discard
- 2 cups of All-purpose Flour
- 1 cup of Grated Sharp Cheddar Cheese
- 1/2 cup of Unsalted Butter, cold and cut into small cubes
- 3/4 cup of Milk
- 2 tsp of Baking Powder
- 1/2 tsp of Baking Soda
- 1/2 tsp of Salt

INSTRUCTIONS:
1. Preheat your oven to 425°F (220°C) and line a baking sheet with parchment paper.
2. In a large bowl, combine the all-purpose flour, baking powder, baking soda, and salt.
3. Add the cold butter to the flour mixture. Use your fingers to work the butter into the flour until the mixture resembles coarse crumbs.
4. Stir in the grated cheddar cheese.
5. Add the sourdough discard and milk to the flour mixture. Stir until just combined, do not overmix. The dough will be sticky.
6. Flour your hands and a clean kitchen surface and turn out the dough onto the surface. Gently pat the dough into a rectangle about 1-inch thick.
7. Using a round biscuit cutter, cut out biscuits from the dough and place them onto the prepared baking sheet. You should get about 8 biscuits.
8. Bake the biscuits for about 20 minutes, until golden brown.
9. Allow the biscuits to cool on the baking sheet for a few minutes, then transfer to a wire rack to cool further.
10. Serve warm with butter or your favorite spread.

CHERRY ALMOND BREAD

Preparation time: 30 minutes
Cooking time: 60 minutes
Servings: 4

INGREDIENTS:
- 2 cups of Sourdough discard
- 1 1/4 cups of All-purpose flour
- 2/3 cup of Sugar
- 1/4 teaspoon of Salt
- 1 teaspoon of baking soda
- 1/2 cup of Unsalted butter (melted and cooled)
- 2 large Eggs
- 1 teaspoon of Almond extract
- 1 1/2 cups of dried Cherries (chopped)

- 3/4 cup of Almonds (roughly chopped)

INSTRUCTIONS:
1. Preheat your oven to 350°F (177°C) and grease a 9x5-inch loaf pan.
2. In a large bowl, combine the flour, sugar, salt, and baking soda. Mix until well combined.
3. In a separate bowl, mix together the sourdough discard, melted butter, eggs, and almond extract.
4. Combine the wet and dry ingredients until the dough is formed.
5. Fold in the chopped dried cherries and chopped almonds until they are evenly distributed throughout the dough.
6. Pour dough into the prepared loaf pan, spreading it out evenly with a spatula.
7. Bake in the preheated oven for 60 minutes or until a toothpick inserted into the middle comes out clean.
8. Let the bread cool on a wire rack for 10 minutes before removing it from the pan. Allow it to cool completely before slicing.
9. Enjoy your Sourdough Discard Cherry Almond Bread for breakfast, snack, or dessert. This bread pairs wonderfully with a cup of coffee or tea.

FOCACCIA

Preparation time: 2 hour 30 minutes

Cooking time: 25 minutes
Servings: 4

INGREDIENTS:
- 1 cup sourdough starter (unfed/discarded)
- 1 1/2 cups lukewarm water
- 3 1/2 cups all-purpose flour
- 1 1/2 teaspoon salt
- 1/2 cup extra virgin olive oil, divided
- 1 tablespoon fresh rosemary, chopped
- 1 tablespoon fresh thyme, chopped
- 1 teaspoon sea salt
- Pinch of dried chili flakes

INSTRUCTIONS:
1. In a large bowl, combine the sourdough starter and lukewarm water. Mix until the starter is dissolved.
2. Add in the flour and salt and stir until a dough forms. Turning onto a floured surface, knead the dough for about 5 minutes, until it's smooth and elastic.
3. Transfer the dough into a greased bowl and cover with a damp cloth. Let it rise in a warm place for 2 hours, or until it has doubled in size.
4. Preheat your oven to 425 degrees F (220 degrees C). Line a baking sheet with parchment paper.
5. Place the dough onto the baking sheet and using your fingers, make dimples in the dough.

6. Brush the dough with half of the olive oil, then sprinkle with the chopped rosemary, thyme, sea salt, and chili flakes.
7. Let the dough rest for 20-30 minutes, allowing it to rise slightly more, then pop it into the oven for 20-25 minutes, or until golden brown.
8. As soon as you remove the focaccia from the oven, brush it with the remaining olive oil. Let it cool for 5-10 minutes before slicing and serving.

GARLIC BREAD

Preparation time: 10 minutes
Cooking time: 15 minutes
Servings: 4

INGREDIENTS:
- 1 cup of ripe sourdough discard
- 2 cups of all-purpose flour
- 1 tablespoon of sugar
- 1 teaspoon of salt
- 1 teaspoon of baking soda
- 1/2 cup of water
- 4 tablespoons of unsalted butter
- 4 cloves of garlic, minced
- 2 teaspoons of dried parsley

INSTRUCTIONS:
1. Start by preheating your oven to 400°F (200°C) and lining a baking tray with parchment paper.
2. In a large bowl, blend together the sourdough discard, flour, sugar, salt, baking soda and water. Knead the mixture until it forms a firm dough.
3. Divide the dough into four equal portions and shape each one into a flat oval. Arrange them on the prepared baking tray.
4. In a small saucepan, melt the butter over medium heat. Once melted, add the minced garlic, stir, and let it cook until it becomes fragrant. Remove the pan from heat and stir in the dried parsley.
5. Now, brush each piece of dough with the garlic butter mixture making sure to evenly distribute it.
6. Put the tray into the preheated oven and bake for about 15 minutes, or until the bread is golden brown and crispy.
7. Remove from oven and let the bread cool slightly before serving.

GARLIC KNOTS

Preparation time: 90 minutes
Cooking time: 20 minutes
Servings: 4

INGREDIENTS:
For the Dough:
- 1/2 Cup of Sourdough Discard (at room temperature)
- 2 1/2 Cups of All-Purpose Flour
- 1 Tablespoon of Granulated Sugar
- 1 1/2 Teaspoon of Instant Yeast
- 1 Teaspoon of Salt

- 1 Cup of Warm Water (105-110 degrees Fahrenheit)
- 2 Tablespoon of Olive Oil

For the Garlic Butter Glaze:
- 1/2 Cup of Unsalted Butter
- 4 Cloves of Garlic, finely minced
- 2 Tablespoons of Freshly Chopped Parsley
- 1 Teaspoon of Salt

INSTRUCTIONS:
1. In a large mixing bowl, combine the flour, sugar, yeast, and salt.
2. Add the sourdough discard, warm water, and olive oil to the dry mixture. Stir until it forms a soft dough.
3. Knead the dough in the bowl until it is smooth and does not stick to the sides (around 10 minutes).
4. Cover the bowl with a clean cloth and set in a warm, draft-free spot for about 60 minutes or until the dough doubles in size.
5. Preheat your oven to 400 degrees Fahrenheit and line a baking sheet with parchment paper.
6. After the dough has risen, turn it out onto a floured surface and divide it into 16 equal pieces.
7. Roll each piece into a rope about 10 inches long, then tie into a knot and place on the prepared baking sheet.
8. Repeat with all pieces, then let them rest for about 10 minutes.

9. While the knots are resting, melt the butter in a small saucepan over medium heat.
10. Add the minced garlic, parsley, and salt to the melted butter, and cook for two to three minutes, or until the butter is infused with garlic.
11. 1Place the knots in the preheated oven and bake for 10 minutes. Brush them with half of the garlic butter, then continue baking for another 10 minutes, until golden brown.
12. 1Once removed from the oven, immediately brush with the remaining garlic butter. Serve warm and enjoy!

HAMBURGER BUNS

Preparation time: 2 hours 30 minutes (includes rising time)
Cooking time: 15-20 minutes
Servings: 4

INGREDIENTS:
- 1 cup Sourdough Discard
- 2 1/2 cups All-purpose Flour
- 1/2 cup Milk
- 1/4 cup Unsalted Butter, at room temperature
- 1 Egg
- 2 tablespoons Sugar
- 1 teaspoon Salt
- 1 tablespoon Active Dry Yeast
- 1 Egg (for egg wash)
- Sesame Seeds (optional)

INSTRUCTIONS:

1. Warm the milk to about 110°F. Mix in the sugar and yeast. Let the mixture sit for about 10 minutes to proof the yeast. It should become frothy.
2. In a large mixing bowl, add the sourdough discard and yeast mixture. Stir in the softened butter, salt, and egg.
3. Gradually add the flour while stirring. The mixture should form a soft, elastic dough.
4. Knead the dough on a well-floured surface until it becomes smooth and no longer sticky. This step can take around 10 minutes.
5. Place the dough in a greased bowl, cover with a cloth and let it rise in a warm place for 2 hours or until it doubles in size.
6. Punch down the dough and divide it into 4 equal parts. Shape each part into a round bun and place it on a baking sheet lined with parchment paper. Allow buns to rise for an additional 30 minutes.
7. Preheat your oven to 375°F. In a small bowl, whisk the second egg and lightly brush it over the top of each bun. If you like, you can sprinkle some sesame seeds on top.
8. Bake the buns for 15-20 minutes or until they are golden brown.
9. Allow the buns to cool before slicing them open.
10. Enjoy your homemade Sourdough Discard Hamburger Buns with your favorite burger recipe!

HERB CRACKERS

Preparation time: 10 minutes
Cooking time: 20 minutes
Servings: 4

INGREDIENTS:
- 1 cup of sourdough discard
- 1 cup of all-purpose flour
- 1/2 cup of olive oil
- 1/2 teaspoon of sea salt
- 1/4 teaspoon of pepper
- 2 teaspoons of mixed herbs (basil, oregano, thyme, rosemary)
- 1/2 teaspoon of garlic powder
- Extra salt for topping

INSTRUCTIONS:
1. Preheat your oven to 350°F (180°C). Line a large baking sheet with parchment paper.
2. In a large mixing bowl, combine the sourdough discard, all-purpose flour, olive oil, sea salt, pepper, mixed herbs, and garlic powder. Stir until all the ingredients are thoroughly mixed together.
3. Take the dough and place it on a piece of lightly floured parchment paper. Roll it out as thin as you can without tearing it. For crisp cracker, the dough should be no more than 1/8-inch thick.
4. Transfer the dough from the parchment paper onto the prepared baking sheet. Sprinkle

the dough with additional salt according to your own taste.

5. Bake in the preheated oven for 20 minutes, or until the crackers are golden brown around the edges. You may need to rotate the baking sheet halfway through cooking for a more even color.

6. Let the crackers cool completely before breaking them into pieces. You can store any leftovers in an airtight container for up to one week.

HOAGIE ROLLS

Preparation time: 25 minutes
Cooking time: 22 minutes
Servings: 4

INGREDIENTS:
- 1 1/2 cups of all-purpose flour
- 1 cup of bread dough
- 1 cup of sourdough discard
- 1/2 tsp of salt
- 2 tsp of sugar
- 1 tsp of active dry yeast
- 1 tbsp of olive oil
- 1/2 cup warm water (110-115°F)

INSTRUCTIONS:
1. In a large bowl, combine the flour, bread dough, sourdough discard, salt, and sugar.

2. Dissolve the yeast in a separate bowl with warm water. Allow it to sit for around five minutes until it starts to froth.

3. Pour the yeast mixture and olive oil into the flour mixture. Stir to combine. The dough should be tacky but not overly sticky.

4. Transfer the dough onto a floured surface and knead for about ten minutes until it becomes smooth and elastic.

5. Form the dough into a ball and place in a greased bowl and cover with a clean cloth. Let it rest in a warm space for around 1 to 1 and a half hours or until it doubles in size.

6. After the dough has risen, punch it down, and divide it into four equal pieces. Form each piece into a log approximately 6 inches long.

7. Preheat your oven to 425°F (220°C) and place a baking stone or upside-down baking dish in the oven to heat.

8. Arrange the dough logs on a floured baking sheet, allowing ample space for expansion. Let them rest for an additional 15 minutes.

9. After the resting time, transfer the rolls gently onto the preheated stone or baking dish in the oven.

10. Bake for 22 minutes, or until the rolls are golden brown and sound hollow when tapped on the bottom.

11. Let rolls cool down before serving. Enjoy your Sourdough Discard Hoagie Rolls with your favorite sandwich fillings!

JALAPENO CHEDDAR BREAD

Preparation time: 150 minutes
Cooking time: 30 minutes
Servings: 4

INGREDIENTS:

- 1 cup sourdough discard
- 3 cups all-purpose flour
- 1 1/4 cups warm water
- 2 teaspoons active dry yeast
- 1 1/2 teaspoons salt
- 1/2 cup shredded sharp cheddar cheese
- 1 large jalapeno, seeded and finely chopped
- 2 tablespoons olive oil
- 2 tablespoons honey
- 1/2 teaspoon garlic powder
- 1 egg (for egg wash before baking)
- Optional: 2 tablespoons cornmeal (for dusting)

INSTRUCTIONS:

1. In a large bowl, combine the warm water and yeast. Allow the mixture to sit for about 5-10 minutes until it becomes frothy.
2. Mix in the sourdough discard, flour, salt, olive oil, honey, and garlic powder. Stir until a sticky dough forms.
3. Turn the dough out onto a lightly floured surface and knead the dough for about 10 minutes, until it feels smooth and elastic.
4. Incorporate the cheese and chopped jalapeno into the dough, ensuring it's evenly distributed.
5. Place the dough into a greased bowl, cover it with a tea towel, and let it rise in a warm place for about 2 hours, or until it doubles in size.
6. Once the dough has risen, preheat your oven to 450 degrees F. If you're using a baking stone, place it in the oven to preheat as well.
7. Turn the dough out onto a lightly floured surface and gently shape it into a round loaf.
8. If using cornmeal, sprinkle it onto a baking sheet or onto your preheated baking stone.
9. Place the loaf onto your prepared surface, cover it with a tea towel, and let it rise for another 30 minutes.
10. Beat the egg and brush it over the top of the loaf. This will give it a glossy finish when baked.
11. Make a few shallow slashes on top of the loaf with a sharp knife, then bake in the preheated oven for about 30 minutes or until the bread is golden brown and sounds hollow when tapped on the bottom.
12. Remove from the oven and allow it to cool on a wire rack before slicing and serving.

MASHED POTATO ROLLS

Preparation time: 60 minutes
Cooking time: 30 minutes
Servings: 4

INGREDIENTS:
- 1 cup of sourdough discard
- 1 small potato (approximately 3/4 cup when mashed)
- 1/4 cup of warm water
- 2 1/4 teaspoons of active dry yeast
- 3 tablespoons of sugar
- 1/4 cup of unsalted butter, melted
- 1 large egg
- 3 cups of all-purpose flour
- 1 teaspoon of salt

INSTRUCTIONS:
1. Start by peeling and cutting the potato into chunks. Place it in a small saucepan with enough water to cover and bring to a boil. Simmer until the potato is tender, about 15 minutes.
2. Drain the water and mash the potato until it's smooth. Let it cool slightly.
3. In a large bowl, combine the warm water and yeast. Let it sit for about 5 minutes, or until the yeast is foamy.
4. Add the mashed potato, sourdough discard, sugar, melted butter, and egg to the bowl. Mix until well combined.
5. Add 2 cups of the flour and the salt to the mixture. Stir until the dough comes together.
6. Turn the dough out onto a floured surface. Knead, gradually adding the remaining flour, until the dough is smooth and elastic. This should take about 8 minutes.
7. Place the dough in a greased bowl, cover with a clean cloth, and let it rise in a warm place until it has doubled in size. This should take about an hour.
8. After the dough has risen, punch it down and divide it into 12 pieces. Shape each piece into a roll.
9. Place the rolls on a greased baking sheet or in a greased muffin tin. Cover and let them rise again for about 30 minutes.
10. Preheat your oven to 375°F (190°C). Bake the rolls for about 25-30 minutes, or until they are golden brown.
11. Serve warm and enjoy your Sourdough Discard Mashed Potato Rolls!

OATMEAL BREAD

Preparation time: 20 minutes
Cooking time: 60 minutes
Servings: 4

INGREDIENTS:
- 1 cup sourdough starter discard
- 2 cups all-purpose flour
- 1 cup old-fashioned rolled oats
- 1/4 cup brown sugar
- 2 teaspoons baking powder
- 1 teaspoon salt
- 1 1/2 cups milk
- 3 tablespoons vegetable oil

INSTRUCTIONS:

1. Preheat your oven to 375°F (190°C). Lightly grease a loaf pan.
2. In a large mixing bowl, combine the sourdough discard, all-purpose flour, rolled oats, brown sugar, baking powder, and salt. Mix until the ingredients are well incorporated.
3. Add the milk and vegetable oil to the bowl. Stir until a sticky dough forms.
4. Transfer the dough into your prepared loaf pan. Use a spatula to smooth the surface of the dough.
5. Bake in the preheated oven for 60 minutes. The bread is done when it's golden brown and a toothpick inserted into the center comes out clean.
6. Let the bread cool in the pan for 10 minutes. Then, remove it from the pan and transfer it to a wire rack to cool completely.
7. Serve as is or slice and toast before serving. Enjoy your Sourdough Discard Oatmeal Bread for breakfast or as a hearty snack.

OLIVE BREAD

Preparation time: 15 minutes
Cooking time: 35 minutes
Servings: 4

INGREDIENTS:
- 2 cups sourdough discard
- 3 cups bread flour
- 1 cup pitted kalamata olives, chopped
- 2 teaspoons salt
- 2 tablespoons olive oil
- 1/2 cup warm water
- 1 teaspoon sugar
- 2 1/4 teaspoons active dry yeast

INSTRUCTIONS:
1. In a large bowl, combine sourdough discard, bread flour, chopped kalamata olives, and salt. Mix thoroughly until all ingredients are well incorporated.
2. In a separate small bowl, mix together the warm water, sugar, and active dry yeast. Allow it to sit for about 5 minutes until the mixture becomes frothy.
3. Add the yeast mixture and olive oil to the dry ingredients. Stir until a sticky dough develops.
4. Turn the dough onto a floured surface and knead it for about 5 minutes. If the dough is too sticky, add a bit more flour.
5. Place the kneaded dough in an oiled bowl and cover with a clean kitchen towel. Allow it to rise in a warm area for approximately 1 hour, or until the dough has doubled in size.
6. Preheat your oven to 375 degrees Fahrenheit.
7. Once the dough has risen, knead it again briefly and shape it into a loaf. Place the loaf on a baking sheet lined with parchment paper.

8. Bake in the preheated oven for about 35 minutes, or until the bread is golden brown and makes a hollow sound when tapped.

9. Allow the bread to cool on a wire rack before slicing and serving with the dish of your choice.

10. Enjoy the unique blend of sourdough discard and olives in this hearty bread! It's a perfect complement to any meal or served alone with a smattering of butter or extra virgin olive oil.

PITA BREAD

Preparation time: 1 hour 30 minutes
Cooking time: 5 minutes
Servings: 4

INGREDIENTS:
- 1 cup of sourdough discard
- 1/2 cup of warm water
- 2 cups of all-purpose flour
- 1 teaspoon of granulated sugar
- 1 tablespoon of olive oil
- 1 teaspoon of salt
- 1/2 teaspoon of instant yeast

INSTRUCTIONS:
1. In a large mixing bowl, combine the sourdough discard and warm water, stirring until it is well combined.

2. In a separate bowl, whisk together the flour, sugar, and instant yeast.

3. Gradually add the flour mixture to the water and sourdough discard mixture, stirring constantly to ensure there are no lumps.

4. Pour in the olive oil, add the salt, and knead the mixture in the bowl until it forms a smooth dough. This process should take about 5-7 minutes.

5. Place the dough ball in a greased bowl, cover with a damp cloth or plastic wrap, and let it rise in a warm place for about 1 hour or until it doubles in size.

6. After the dough has risen, preheat your oven to 500 degrees F (260 degrees C) and place a baking stone or heavy baking sheet in the oven to heat.

7. Divide the dough into 8 even pieces and flatten each piece into a circle approximately 6 inches in diameter.

8. Transfer the dough circles onto the hot baking stone or sheet in the oven, baking for about 2-3 minutes on each side or until puffed up and lightly golden.

9. Remove the cooked pita bread from the oven and let them cool on a wire rack before serving.

PIZZA CRUST

Preparation time: 2 hours
Cooking time: 20 minutes
Servings: 4

INGREDIENTS:
- 2 cups of sourdough starter discard
- 3 cups of all-purpose flour

- 1 teaspoon of salt
- 1 teaspoon of sugar
- 2 tablespoons of olive oil
- 1 cup of warm water
- 2 1/4 teaspoons of active dry yeast (1 packet)

INSTRUCTIONS:

1. Begin by proofing the yeast. In a small bowl, combine the warm water and sugar, stirring until the sugar is dissolved. Sprinkle the yeast on top of the water and let sit for about 5 minutes. You should see some bubbles forming on top.
2. In a separate large bowl, combine the flour and salt. Make a well in the center and add the oil, the proofed yeast mixture, and the sourdough discard.
3. Using a dough hook or your hands, mix the ingredients together until a dough forms. If it's too dry, add a little more water, a tablespoon at a time. If it's too wet, add more flour.
4. Once the dough has come together, knead it on a lightly floured surface for about 10 minutes. It should be smooth and elastic when you're done.
5. Place the dough in a greased bowl, cover it with a clean kitchen towel, and let it rise in a warm place for about 1-1.5 hours, or until it has doubled in size.
6. Preheat your oven to 450°F (232°C). If you have a pizza

stone, put it in the oven while it preheats.
7. Punch down the dough and divide it into 4 equal pieces. Roll out each piece on a floured surface until it's about 1/4 inch thick.
8. If you're using a pizza stone, transfer one of the rolled-out pieces of dough onto a pizza peel or an inverted baking sheet dusted with flour.
9. Add your toppings of choice and then carefully transfer the pizza from the peel or baking sheet to the preheated stone in the oven. If you're not using a pizza stone, you can simply place your rolled-out dough onto a greased or parchment-lined baking sheet, add your toppings, and then put it in the oven.
10. Bake for about 12-15 minutes, or until the crust is golden and the cheese (if used) is bubbly and starting to turn brown.
11. Repeat with the remaining pieces of dough.

POTATO BREAD

Preparation time: 20 minutes
Cooking time: 40 minutes
Servings: 4

INGREDIENTS:
- 2 cups of sourdough discard
- 2 medium-sized russet potatoes
- 1 tablespoon salt
- 3 cups of all-purpose flour

- 1 packet (about 2 1/4 teaspoons) of active dry yeast
- 1 tablespoon white sugar
- 2 tablespoons of olive oil
- 1/4 cup of warm water (around 110 degrees F)

INSTRUCTIONS:

1. Start by peeling and dicing the potatoes. Then, boil them in a pot over medium heat until they are soft. This should take approximately 15 minutes.
2. Once the potatoes are cooked, drain them, and keep the potato water. Measure 1 cup of this potato water, allow it to cool and then dissolve the yeast and sugar into it. Wait for about 10 minutes until the mixture looks foamy.
3. Mash the potatoes in a separate bowl. Combine the mashed potatoes, sourdough discard, salt, and olive oil in a large bowl.
4. Gradually add in the flour to this potato mixture. Then pour in the yeast-potato water mixture. Stir everything together until a dough begins to form.
5. Knead the dough on a floured surface for about 10 minutes until it becomes smooth and elastic. If the dough is too sticky, add more flour.
6. Place the dough in a greased bowl, cover it with plastic wrap and let it rise until it doubles in size. This will take around 1 to 1.5 hours.

7. After it has risen, punch down the dough and knead it a few more times. Shape it into a loaf and place it in a greased loaf pan.
8. Preheat your oven to 375 degrees F. While the oven is preheating, let the dough rise in the pan for about 30 minutes.
9. Once the dough has risen, bake the loaf in the preheated oven for 35 to 40 minutes until it is golden brown.
10. Allow the bread to cool before serving and enjoy your Sourdough Discard Potato Bread!

PUMPERNICKEL BREAD

Preparation time: 20 minutes
Cooking time: 40 minutes
Forming and resting time: 4 hours
Servings: 4

INGREDIENTS:

- 1 1/2 cups of sourdough discard
- 2 cups of bread flour
- 1/2 cup of rye flour
- 2 tablespoons of unsweetened cocoa powder
- 2 tablespoons of caraway seeds
- 1 tablespoon of salt
- 2 tablespoons of molasses
- 1/2 cup of warm water (for yeast mixture)
- 2 teaspoons of active dry yeast
- 1 tablespoon of sugar

INSTRUCTIONS:

1. Start by combining your active dry yeast, sugar, and warm water

in a small bowl. Set aside for 5 minutes, allowing the mixture to become foamy.

2. In a large bowl, add your sourdough discard, bread flour, rye flour, unsweetened cocoa powder, caraway seeds, and salt. Stir well to combine.

3. Add the molasses to your yeast mixture, then pour this wet mixture into the larger bowl with the dry ingredients. Stir until all the ingredients are well incorporated and a sticky dough forms.

4. Turn the dough out onto a lightly floured surface and knead for about 10 minutes, or until the dough is smooth and elastic.

5. Place the dough into a greased bowl, covering with a cloth. Let it rise until it has doubled in size, which should take about 2 hours.

6. Once risen, punch down the dough and knead it a few times. Shape it into a loaf and place it in a greased loaf pan. Let the dough rest and rise for another 2 hours.

7. Preheat your oven to 375°F. Bake the bread for about 40 minutes, or until the top is browned and the loaf sounds hollow when tapped on the bottom.

8. Let the bread cool in the pan for about 10 minutes, then remove to cool completely on a wire rack.

9. Slice and serve your sourdough discard pumpernickel bread

warm or at room temperature. Enjoy with a slab of butter or your favorite bread spread.

PUMPKIN BREAD

Preparation time: 20 minutes
Cooking time: 60 minutes
Servings: 4

INGREDIENTS:

1. 1 cup sourdough starter discard
2. 1 cup pumpkin puree
3. 1 cup granulated sugar
4. 1/2 cup vegetable oil
5. 2 large eggs
6. 1 1/2 cups all-purpose flour
7. 1 teaspoon baking soda
8. 1/2 teaspoon baking powder
9. 1/2 teaspoon salt
10. 2 teaspoons pumpkin spice
11. 11/2 teaspoon vanilla extract

INSTRUCTIONS:

1. Preheat your oven to 350°F (175°C). Lightly grease a 9-inch loaf pan and put aside.
2. In a large bowl, mix together the sourdough starter discard, pumpkin puree, sugar, oil, and eggs until well combined.
3. In a separate bowl, whisk together the flour, baking soda, baking powder, salt, and pumpkin spice.
4. Gradually add the dry ingredients to the wet ingredients, mixing just until combined.
5. Stir in the vanilla extract.

6. Pour the batter into the prepared loaf pan, smoothing the top with a spatula.
7. Bake in the preheated oven for about 60 minutes, or until a toothpick inserted into the center comes out clean.
8. Let the bread cool in the pan for 10 minutes, then turn it out onto a wire rack to cool completely.
9. Slice and serve your Sourdough Discard Pumpkin Bread while it's still warm. Enjoy the rich, spiced flavors with a touch of sourdough tang.

QUICK BREAD

Preparation time: 15 minutes
Cooking time: 45 minutes
Servings: 4

INGREDIENTS:
- 1 cup of sourdough starter discard
- 3 cups of all-purpose flour
- 2 tablespoons of sugar
- 1 cup of warm water (not exceeding 110°F)
- 1 teaspoon of salt
- 2 teaspoons of baking soda
- Vegan or normal butter for greasing (optional)

INSTRUCTIONS:
1. Preheat your oven to 375°F (190°C). Grease your bread pan with butter to avoid the bread sticking to the pan.
2. In a large mixing bowl, combine the sourdough discard, all-purpose flour, sugar, salt, and baking soda. Mix everything together until the ingredients are evenly distributed.
3. Slowly add the warm water to the mixture, stirring continuously. You want the consistency to be a thick, sticky dough. Don't worry about it being smooth as it doesn't need to be kneaded.
4. Once the dough is mixed, transfer it straight into your greased bread pan. If desired, you can smooth the top with a spatula, but this isn't necessary.
5. Place the pan in the oven and bake for approximately 45 minutes, or until the bread has a golden-brown crust and a skewer inserted into the centre comes out clean.
6. Remove the bread from the oven and allow it to cool in the pan for about 10 minutes. Then, remove it from the pan and let it cool completely on a wire rack before slicing and serving.

QUINOA BREAD

Preparation time: 2 hours
Cooking time: 45 minutes
Servings: 4

INGREDIENTS:
- 1 cup of sourdough discard
- 1 cup of cooked quinoa
- 2 cups of bread flour

- 1/2 cup of water
- 1 tablespoon of sugar
- 2 teaspoons of quick-rising yeast
- 1/2 teaspoon of salt
- 2 tablespoons of olive oil

INSTRUCTIONS:
1. In a large bowl, combine the sourdough discard and cooked quinoa. Mix until well combined.
2. In a separate bowl, combine the bread flour, sugar, yeast, and salt. Stir well.
3. Gradually add the dry ingredients into the bowl with the wet ingredients. Add the water gradually, beginning with 1/4 cup, and adding more as needed. Mix until the dough starts to come together.
4. Once the dough has formed, transfer it onto a floured surface and knead for about 10 minutes, or until the dough is smooth and elastic. Add more flour if the dough is too wet or sticky.
5. Place the dough in a greased bowl and cover with a clean towel. Let it rise for about 1 hour, or until it has doubled in size.
6. After the dough has risen, punch it down to release the air. Transfer the dough to a greased loaf pan and cover again. Allow it to rise for another hour.
7. Preheat your oven to 375 degrees F (190 degrees C). Once the dough has risen, place the loaf pan in the preheated oven.

8. Bake for 40-45 minutes, or until the bread is golden brown and sounds hollow when tapped on the bottom.
9. Remove from oven and let it cool on a wire rack before slicing and serving.

RYE BREAD

Preparation time: 25 minutes
Cooking time: 35 minutes
Servings: 4

INGREDIENTS:
- 1 cup sourdough discard
- 2 cups rye flour
- 1 cup all-purpose flour
- 1 1/2 cups warm water
- 2 teaspoons active dry yeast
- 1 tablespoon sugar
- 2 tablespoons olive oil
- 1 1/2 teaspoons salt
- 2 teaspoons caraway seeds (optional)

INSTRUCTIONS:
1. In a large bowl, combine the sourdough discard with the warm water. Stir until the discard is fully dissolved.
2. Add the active dry yeast and sugar to the bowl. Give it a good stir to combine and let the mixture sit for 5-10 minutes until it's frothy.
3. In another bowl, combine the rye flour, all-purpose flour, and salt. Mix until well combined.

4. Gradually add the dry mixture to the wet, stirring continuously until a thick dough forms. If using, add in the caraway seeds at this step.
5. Drizzle olive oil over the dough and knead in the bowl for about 5 minutes, until the dough becomes smooth and elastic.
6. Cover the bowl with a clean towel and place it in a warm, draft-free area for 2-3 hours, or until the dough has doubled in size.
7. Preheat your oven to 450°F (230°C) and line a baking tray with parchment paper.
8. Once the dough has risen, punch it down and shape it into a loaf. Place the loaf onto your prepared tray.
9. Bake in the preheated oven for about 35 minutes, or until the crust is golden brown and sounds hollow when tapped on the bottom.
10. Allow the bread to cool before slicing and enjoying.

SOURDOUGH DISCARD BISCUITS

Preparation time: 20 minutes
Cooking time: 15 minutes
Servings: 4

INGREDIENTS:
- 1 cup of sourdough starter discard
- 2 cups of all-purpose flour (plus extra for dusting)
- 1 tablespoon of sugar
- 3 teaspoons of baking powder
- 1 teaspoon of salt
- 1/2 cup (1 stick) of unsalted butter, very cold and cut into small cubes
- 1/2 cup of milk

INSTRUCTIONS:
1. Preheat your oven to 425°F(220°C) and line a baking sheet with parchment paper.
2. In a large bowl, combine the flour, sugar, baking powder, and salt.
3. Add the cold butter to the flour mixture. Use your fingers or a pastry cutter to cut the butter into the flour until it resembles coarse breadcrumbs.
4. Pour in the sourdough starter discard and milk. Stir until just combined. Do not overmix, or your biscuits may become tough.
5. On a well-floured surface, turn out the dough and pat it into a rectangle, about 1-inch thick.
6. Using a round biscuit cutter, cut out biscuits from the dough and place them on the prepared baking sheet.
7. Bake for around 15 minutes, or until the biscuits have risen and are golden brown on top.
8. Remove from the oven and let them cool slightly before serving.

SWEET POTATO BREAD

Preparation time: 20 minutes
Cooking time: 50 minutes

Servings: 4

INGREDIENTS:
- 1 cup of sourdough discard
- 1 cup of mashed sweet potato
- 2 eggs
- 1/2 cup of brown sugar
- 1/4 cup of vegetable oil
- 1 tsp of vanilla extract
- 1 1/2 cups of all-purpose flour
- 1/2 tsp of baking powder
- 1/2 tsp of baking soda
- 1/2 tsp of salt
- 1 tsp of ground cinnamon
- 1/2 tsp of ground nutmeg

INSTRUCTIONS:
1. Preheat the oven to 350°F (177°C) and grease a 9x5-inch loaf pan.
2. In a large bowl, combine the sourdough discard, mashed sweet potato, eggs, brown sugar, vegetable oil, and vanilla extract. Mix well until everything is fully combined.
3. In another bowl, combine the all-purpose flour, baking powder, baking soda, salt, ground cinnamon, and ground nutmeg. Stir until well mixed.
4. Gradually add the dry ingredients to the wet ingredients, mixing just until combined. Be careful not to over mix.
5. Pour the batter into the prepared loaf pan and smooth the top with the back of a spoon or spatula.
6. Bake for 50-60 minutes, or until a toothpick inserted into the center of the bread comes out clean. If the bread is browning too much and still isn't finished baking, loosely cover with foil, and continue to bake until done.
7. Allow the bread to cool in the pan on a wire rack for 10 minutes, then remove from the pan and allow it to cool completely on the wire rack.
8. Slice, serve, and enjoy your Sourdough Discard Sweet Potato Bread!

WHOLE WHEAT BREAD

Preparation time: 120 minutes
Cooking time: 30 minutes
Servings: 4

INGREDIENTS:
- 1 1/2 cups of sourdough discard
- 2 cups of whole wheat flour
- 2 teaspoons of salt
- 1 tablespoon of white sugar
- 1 tablespoon of olive oil
- 3/4 cup of lukewarm water
- 1/2 teaspoon of instant yeast

INSTRUCTIONS:
1. In a large mixing bowl, combine the sourdough discard, whole wheat flour, salt, and sugar. Mix it until it's well combined.
2. Add the olive oil, lukewarm water, and instant yeast into the dry ingredients. Stir it continually until it forms into dough.
3. Knead the dough on a floured surface for about 5-10 minutes

until it becomes smooth and elastic.

4. Form the dough into a ball and put it back into the bowl. Cover it with a clean kitchen towel and let it rise within 1 to 2 hours until it doubles in size.

5. After the dough has risen, punch it down and reshape it into a loaf. Place it on a lightly greased loaf pan.

6. Preheat the oven to 375°F (190°C). While the oven preheats, let the dough rise again for another 20-30 minutes.

7. Once the oven is preheated, put the loaf pan in the oven and bake it for 30 minutes or until the top becomes golden brown and the loaf sounds hollow when tapped on the bottom.

8. Take the loaf out of the oven and let it cool on a wire rack.

9. After it cools completely, cut it into slices and serve.

SAVORY SNACKS

CHEESE STRAWS

Preparation time: 15 minutes
Cooking time: 15 minutes
Servings: 4

INGREDIENTS:
- 2 cups of all-purpose flour
- 3/4 cup of cold, unsalted butter cut into small cubes
- 1 cup of shredded sharp cheddar cheese
- 1/2 cup of sourdough starter discard
- 1/4 tsp of salt
- 1/4 tsp cayenne pepper (optional)
- 2 tbsp of water (only if needed)
- Coarse salt for sprinkling

INSTRUCTIONS:
1. Preheat your oven to 375°F (190°C) and line a baking sheet with parchment paper.
2. In a large bowl, combine the flour, cubed butter, shredded cheddar, sourdough discard, salt, and cayenne pepper. Using your fingers, rub the butter into the flour until it resembles coarse crumbs.
3. Continue to mix until you've formed a dough that holds together when squeezed. If the dough is too dry, gradually add the water until the desired consistency is achieved.
4. Roll the dough between two sheets of parchment paper until it's about 1/8 inch thick. Trim the edges to make a rectangle and then cut the dough into thin strips, about 1/2 inch wide.
5. Transfer the strips to the prepared baking sheet, press them lightly with a fork to make ridges, and sprinkle with coarse salt.
6. Bake for 13-15 minutes, or until the cheese straws are a light golden brown.
7. Let the cheese straws cool completely on the baking sheet before serving them, this will also allow them to crisp up.

CRAB CAKES

Preparation time: 20 minutes
Cooking time: 10 minutes
Servings: 4

INGREDIENTS:
- 1 cup of Sourdough Discard
- 1 pound of fresh Crab Meat
- 1/2 cup of Breadcrumbs, preferably Panko
- 1 large Egg
- 2 tablespoons of Mayonnaise
- 1 teaspoon of Dijon mustard
- 1 teaspoon of Old Bay Seasoning, or to taste
- 2 green Onions, finely chopped
- 1/4 cup of fresh Parsley, finely chopped
- Salt and Pepper to taste
- Vegetable Oil for frying
- Lemon wedges for serving

INSTRUCTIONS:

1. In a large bowl, mix together the sourdough discard, crab meat, breadcrumbs, egg, mayonnaise, Dijon mustard, Old Bay seasoning, green onions, and parsley. Season with salt and pepper.
2. Using your hands, form the mixture into eight patties and place them on a plate. Cover the plate with plastic wrap and refrigerate the patties for at least 1 hour. This will help them retain their shape as they cook.
3. Preheat a large skillet over medium-high heat and add enough vegetable oil to reach about 1/2-inch up the sides.
4. Once the oil is hot, add the crab cakes and cook for about 4 minutes on each side, until they're golden brown and cooked through.
5. Remove the crab cakes from the skillet and drain on paper towels.
6. Serve the Sourdough Discard Crab Cakes warm, with lemon wedges on the side for squeezing over top.
7. Enjoy this delicious and sustainable use of your sourdough discard!

DUMPLINGS

Preparation time: 20 minutes
Cooking time: 10 minutes
Servings: 4

INGREDIENTS:

- 1 cup sourdough discard
- 2 cups all-purpose flour
- 1/2 cup whole milk or buttermilk
- 2 teaspoons baking powder
- 1/2 teaspoon salt
- 1/4 cup melted unsalted butter
- 1 large egg
- Optional: 2 tablespoons fresh chopped herbs like parsley or thyme

INSTRUCTIONS:
1. In a large bowl, mix together the sourdough discard, flour, baking powder, and salt.
2. In another bowl, whisk together the melted butter and egg. Then, stir in the milk or buttermilk.
3. Pour the wet ingredients into the dry ingredients and stir until it forms a slightly sticky dough. If you'd like to add herbs, stir them in now.
4. With floured hands, form the dough into small balls about the size of a golf ball. Place them on a plate or baking sheet until ready to cook.
5. To cook the dumplings, bring your soup or stew to a gentle boil. Drop in the dumplings one at a time, making sure they do not stick to each other.
6. Reduce the heat to a simmer, cover the pot, and let the dumplings cook for about 10 minutes or until they are puffy and cooked through.
7. Serve the dumplings warm by scooping them out with a slotted

spoon and serving on top of your soup or stew. Enjoy your homemade sourdough discard dumplings.

EMPANADAS

Preparation time: 45 minutes
Cooking time: 20 minutes
Servings: 4

INGREDIENTS:
For the empanada dough:
- 1 cup of sourdough discard
- 2.5 cups of all-purpose flour
- 1 teaspoon of salt
- 1/2 cup of unsalted butter, cold and cubed
- 1/2 cup of cold water

For the filling (vegetable):
- 1 small onion, finely chopped
- 1 bell pepper, finely chopped
- 2 cloves of garlic, minced
- 1 small zucchini, diced
- 1/2 cup of sweet corn
- Salt and pepper to taste
- 1 teaspoon of cumin
- 1 teaspoon of paprika
- 1 tablespoon of olive oil

For the filling (meat):
- 1 small onion, finely chopped
- 2 cloves of garlic, minced
- 1/2-pound ground beef
- Salt and pepper to taste
- 1 teaspoon of cumin
- 1 teaspoon of paprika
- 1 tablespoon of olive oil

INSTRUCTIONS:
1. Start with the empanada dough: In a large bowl, mix together the flour and salt. Add in the butter and use your fingers to cut it into the flour until the mixture resembles coarse breadcrumbs. Stir in the sourdough discard and then gradually mix in cold water until a dough forms. Wrap the dough in plastic and refrigerate for at least 30 minutes.
2. Make your chosen filling: Heat olive oil over medium heat in a frying pan. Add onions and cook until they soften, followed by the garlic. Cook for about one minute, then add your vegetables or meat along with the spices. Cook thoroughly until your meat is browned or your vegetables are tender. Season with salt and pepper and let the mixture cool.
3. Preheat your oven to 375°F (190°C) and line a baking sheet with parchment paper.
4. Divide the dough into 8 pieces. Roll each piece into a thin circle. Place a spoonful of your filling in the center of each circle, then fold the dough over the filling to create a half-moon shape. Press the edges together to seal and crimp the edges with a fork for decoration.
5. Place empanadas on your baking sheet. If desired, brush the pastries with an egg wash for color.

6. Bake for 20-25 minutes or until golden brown and serve warm.

FLATBREAD

Preparation time: 70 minutes
Cooking time: 10 minutes
Servings: 4

INGREDIENTS:
- 1 cup of sourdough starter discard
- 1 cup of all-purpose flour
- 1/2 tsp of salt
- 1/2 tsp of baking powder
- 2 tbsp of olive oil

For Toppings: (optional)
- Sesame seeds
- Fresh herbs (such as thyme, rosemary, or parsley)
- Parmesan cheese

INSTRUCTIONS:
1. In a large bowl, combine your sourdough discard, flour, salt, and baking powder. Stir together until all ingredients are well combined.
2. Pour 1 tablespoon of olive oil into the bowl and knead the mixture until it forms a soft but sticky dough. Add the other tablespoon of olive oil if needed, the dough should be supple but not too sticky.
3. Cover the dough with a clean dishcloth and let it rest at room temperature for about 60 minutes. This resting period allows the dough to rise slightly and will yield a softer flatbread.
4. Preheat your oven to 450 degrees Fahrenheit and place a large baking sheet in to warm up.
5. After resting, divide your dough into 4 equal portions. Using your hands or a rolling pin, shape each portion into a round, flat disk, about 1/4 inch thick.
6. Carefully remove your preheated baking sheet from the oven. Place your dough disks onto the sheet.
7. If you're using toppings, sprinkle them onto the flatbreads now.
8. Bake your flatbreads for about 10 minutes, or until they're lightly golden and crisp.
9. Remove flatbreads from the oven and let them cool on the baking sheet for a minute or two before serving.

FRIED PICKLES

Preparation time: 15 minutes
Cooking time: 20 minutes
Servings: 4

INGREDIENTS:
- 1 cup of sourdough starter discard
- 1 cup of all-purpose flour
- 1/2 cup of buttermilk
- 1 teaspoon of paprika
- 1 teaspoon of garlic powder
- 1/2 teaspoon of salt
- 1/4 teaspoon of black pepper

- 1 jar (16 ounces) of dill pickle slices, drained
- Vegetable oil for frying

INSTRUCTIONS:
1. In a large mixing bowl, combine your sourdough discard and flour. Mix until it forms a pancake-like batter.
2. Stir in your buttermilk. This should create a nice thick batter, but if it's too thick, add a little more buttermilk until you reach your desired consistency.
3. Add the paprika, garlic powder, salt, and black pepper to the batter. Stir until all the ingredients are well incorporated.
4. Heat the vegetable oil in a deep fryer or large deep pan over medium-high heat. You will want to have about 1-2 inches of oil.
5. Dip each pickle slice into the batter, making sure to get a good even coat of batter on all sides.
6. Carefully drop the battered pickles into the hot oil. Fry for a few minutes on each side until they turn golden brown.
7. Use a slotted spoon to remove the fried pickles from the oil and transfer them to a paper towel-lined plate. This will help to drain off any excess oil.
8. Let the pickles cool slightly and serve warm. These tangy, crispy Sourdough Discard Fried Pickles make an amazing snack or side for any meal.

9. Remember to enjoy the unique tang that the sourdough discard brings to the batter!

KALE CHIPS

Preparation time: 10 minutes
Cooking time: 25 minutes
Servings: 4

INGREDIENTS:
- 2 large bunches of Kale
- ½ cup of Sourdough Discard
- 2 tablespoons Olive Oil
- 1 teaspoon Garlic Powder
- ½ teaspoon Salt
- ¼ teaspoon Black Pepper

INSTRUCTIONS:
1. Preheat your oven to 300°F and line two large baking sheets with parchment paper.
2. Thoroughly wash the kale and dry it completely before removing the tough stems. Tear the leaves into large pieces, they will shrink in the oven.
3. In a large bowl, combine the sourdough discard, olive oil, garlic powder, salt, and pepper. Add the kale leaves to the bowl and use your hands to massage the mixture into the kale, ensuring each piece is evenly coated.
4. Lay the kale out in a single layer on your prepared baking sheets. It's important to avoid overcrowding the kale on the baking sheets, otherwise the kale

chips will steam instead of becoming crisp.

5. Bake in the preheated oven for about 25 minutes or until the kale chips are crisp and the edges are slightly browned.

6. Allow the chips to cool on the baking sheets for about 3 minutes. They will continue to crisp up as they cool.

7. Enjoy your Sourdough Discard Kale Chips immediately for the best flavor and texture.

8. Leftovers can be stored in an airtight container at room temperature for up to 5 days.

MOZZARELLA STICKS

Preparation time: 30 minutes
Cooking time: 10 minutes
Servings: 4

INGREDIENTS:
- 16 Mozzarella sticks
- 1 cup Sourdough discard
- 1 cup Plain flour
- 2 Eggs
- 2 cups Breadcrumbs, seasoned for preference
- 1 tsp Salt
- 1/2 tsp Black pepper
- Cooking oil, for frying
- Marinara sauce, for dipping (optional)

INSTRUCTIONS:
1. First, freeze the mozzarella sticks for about 1-2 hours until they are very firm.

2. Now, set up a breading station. In a shallow dish, add plain flour. In a second dish, whisk the eggs. In the third dish, mix together the breadcrumbs, sourdough discard, salt, and black pepper.

3. Remove the mozzarella sticks from the freezer. Roll each in the flour, then dip in the beaten eggs, allowing any excess to drip off. After that, roll in the sourdough discard breadcrumb mixture making sure they're well coated.

4. Place breaded mozzarella sticks back in the freezer for about 15 minutes. This will help the breading to adhere to the cheese sticks and helps them hold their shape when fried.

5. Fill a deep pan with about two inches of cooking oil. Heat over medium-high heat until the oil reaches around 375°F.

6. Working in batches, fry the mozzarella sticks until golden brown. This should take about 2-3 minutes. Keep an eye on them, as they can quickly go from golden to burnt.

7. Once fried, remove the sticks using a slotted spoon and let them drain on a paper towel-lined plate.

8. Allow to cool for a few minutes before serving.

ONION RINGS

Preparation time: 20 minutes
Cooking time: 10 minutes

Servings: 4

INGREDIENTS:
- 3 large onions, sliced into 1/2-inch rings
- 1 cup sourdough discard
- 1 cup all-purpose flour
- 1/2 cup cornmeal
- 1 and 1/2 cups buttermilk
- 1 teaspoon baking powder
- 1/2 teaspoon baking soda
- 1/2 teaspoon salt
- 1/2 teaspoon paprika
- 1/2 teaspoon garlic powder
- Vegetable oil, for frying

INSTRUCTIONS:
1. Cut the onions into 1/2-inch rings and separate the rings.
2. In a large bowl, combine sourdough discard, all-purpose flour, cornmeal, buttermilk, baking powder, baking soda, salt, and spices to create your batter. Mix until well combined.
3. Heat 2-3 inches of vegetable oil in a deep fryer or large saucepan to 375°F (190°C). Use a thermometer to ensure the accurate temperature.
4. Dip each onion ring into the batter, ensuring each ring is fully coated. Carefully place a few rings into the hot oil.
5. Fry the onion rings until golden brown, about 2-3 minutes on each side. Be sure not to crowd the pan, work in batches if necessary.
6. Use a slotted spoon to remove the onion rings from the oil and drain them on a plate lined with paper towels.
7. Serve immediately while warm and enjoy the crispy, golden onion rings with the tang from sourdough batter. Experiment with dipping sauces for added flavor.

PARMESAN CRACKERS

Preparation time: 15 minutes
Cooking time: 15 minutes
Servings: 4

INGREDIENTS:
- 1 cup of sourdough discard
- 1 cup of all-purpose flour
- 1/3 cup of freshly grated parmesan cheese
- 1/4 cup of unsalted butter, at room temperature
- 1/2 teaspoon of sea salt
- 1/4 teaspoon of garlic powder
- 1/4 teaspoon black pepper

INSTRUCTIONS:
1. Start by preheating your oven to 350°F (175°C) and lining a baking sheet with a piece of parchment paper.
2. In a large mixing bowl, combine the sourdough discard, all-purpose flour, freshly grated parmesan cheese, unsalted butter, sea salt, garlic powder, and black pepper.

3. Use a food processor or your hands to mix the ingredients together until a dough forms.
4. Turn the dough out onto a lightly floured work surface and roll out the dough until it's approximately 1/8 inch thick.
5. Using a pizza cutter or a sharp knife, cut the dough into your desired cracker shapes. Transfer the pieces onto the prepared baking sheet.
6. Bake the crackers in the preheated oven for about 15 minutes, or until the edges begin to turn golden brown.
7. Allow the crackers to cool on the baking sheet for few minutes before transferring them to a wire rack to continue cooling.
8. Once completely cooled, serve the sourdough discard parmesan crackers as a snack or with your favorite dish.

POPOVERS

Preparation time: 15 minutes
Cooking time: 35 minutes
Servings: 4

INGREDIENTS:
- 2 cups of sourdough discard
- 1 cup all-purpose flour
- 1/2 cup whole milk, room temperature
- 2 large eggs, room temperature
- 1/2 teaspoon of salt
- 2 tablespoons of unsalted butter, melted

INSTRUCTIONS:
1. First, preheat your oven to 450 degrees Fahrenheit and position a rack in the middle.
2. Next, whisk the eggs and milk together in a medium-sized bowl until they're well-combined.
3. In another bowl, combine the sourdough discard, flour, and salt. Mix until it's smooth.
4. Gradually, add in the milk and egg mixture into the discard flour mixture. Stir until everything is just combined. You want to avoid over-stirring, as that can make the popovers tough. The batter should be thinner than a typical pancake batter.
5. Take your melted butter and lightly brush the insides of a muffin tin or, if you have one, a popover pans.
6. Fill each cup in your tin to about two-thirds full of the popover batter.
7. Place the tin in the oven and bake for 20 minutes. Then, without opening the oven door, reduce the heat to 350 degrees Fahrenheit and continue to bake for 15 more minutes. The popovers should be golden brown and puffed up.
8. Remove the popovers from the oven and let them cool for about 5 minutes in the tin. Then, remove the popovers from the tin and serve immediately for best results. They should be light,

puffy bread rolls with a slight sourdough tang and a delightful hollow center. Enjoy!

PRETZELS

Preparation time: 90 minutes
Cooking time: 15 minutes
Servings: 4

INGREDIENTS:
- 1 cup of sourdough starter discard
- 2 cups of all-purpose flour
- 1 tablespoon of brown sugar
- 1 teaspoon of sea salt
- 1 tablespoon of unsalted butter, melted
- 8 cups of water for boiling the pretzels
- 1/2 cup of baking soda
- 1 large egg (for egg wash)
- Coarse salt for sprinkling

INSTRUCTIONS:
1. Place the sourdough starter discard, all-purpose flour, brown sugar, sea salt, and melted butter in a large mixing bowl. Stir until it forms a dough.
2. Knead the dough on a floured surface for about 10 minutes until it is smooth and elastic, adding more flour if needed.
3. Form the dough into a ball, place it back in the bowl, cover with a damp cloth, and let it rise for about an hour in a warm place until it has doubled in size.
4. Preheat your oven to 425°F (220°C).
5. Divide the dough into 8 pieces. Roll each piece into a rope, twist into a pretzel shape, and place on a parchment-lined baking sheet.
6. In a large pot, bring the 8 cups of water and baking soda to a rolling boil. Boil each pretzel for about 30 seconds per side, then remove with a slotted spoon and place back on the baking sheet.
7. Beat the egg in a small bowl and brush each pretzel with the egg wash, then sprinkle with the coarse salt.
8. Bake for 12-15 minutes until the pretzels are golden brown.
9. Allow to cool on a wire rack for a few minutes before serving.

SAUSAGE ROLLS

Preparation time: 20 minutes
Cooking time: 35 minutes
Servings: 4

INGREDIENTS:
For the pastry:
- 1 cup of sourdough discard
- 2 cups of all-purpose flour
- 1 teaspoon of salt
- 1 cup of ice-cold unsalted butter, cubed
- 3 tablespoons of ice water

For the filling:
- 1 lb of sausage meat
- 1 medium onion, finely chopped

- 2 cloves of garlic, minced
- 1 teaspoon of dried thyme
- Salt and pepper to taste

For the glaze:
- 1 large egg, beaten

INSTRUCTIONS:
1. Start by making your pastry. In a large bowl, combine the sourdough discard, flour, and salt.
2. Add the cubed butter. Rub it in with your fingers until the mixture resembles coarse breadcrumbs.
3. Gradually add ice water, mixing until the dough just comes together.
4. Form the dough into a disc, wrap in cling film, and refrigerate for at least one hour.
5. While the dough is chilling, prepare your filling. In a large frying pan, cook the sausage meat over medium heat, breaking it up into small pieces.
6. Add the onion, garlic, thyme, salt, and pepper. Continue to cook until the onion is soft, and the sausage is fully cooked.
7. Remove from heat and allow to cool slightly.
8. Preheat your oven to 375°F (190°C). Line a baking sheet with parchment paper.
9. On a lightly floured surface, roll out your dough to a thickness of about 1/8 inch.
10. Cut the dough into rectangles approximately 3x4 inches. Spoon some of the sausage mixture onto one half of each rectangle, leaving space around the edges.
11. Fold the dough over the sausage filling, pressing the edges together to seal. Crimp the edges with a fork.
12. Place the sausage rolls on the prepared baking sheet. Cut small slits in the top of each roll to allow steam to escape.
13. Brush each sausage rolls with the beaten egg.
14. Bake for 25-30 minutes, or until golden brown.
15. Allow to cool slightly before serving. Enjoy these savory Sourdough Discard Sausage Rolls.

SAVORY MUFFINS

Preparation time: 15 minutes
Cooking time: 20 minutes
Servings: 4

INGREDIENTS:
- 1 cup of sourdough starter discard
- 1 1/2 cups of all-purpose flour
- 2 tsp of baking powder
- 1/2 tsp of baking soda
- 1/2 tsp of salt
- 1/4 cup of granulated sugar
- 1/4 cup of unsalted butter, melted
- 2 large eggs
- 1/2 cup of whole milk
- 1/2 cup of sharp cheddar cheese, shredded

- 1/4 cup of spring onions, finely chopped
- 1/4 cup of cooked bacon, crumbled

INSTRUCTIONS:

1. Preheat your oven to 375°F (190°C). Line a muffin tin with paper liners or grease it well.
2. In a large bowl, combine the flour, baking powder, baking soda, salt, and sugar. Stir until these dry ingredients are well combined.
3. In a separate bowl, whisk together the sourdough discard, melted butter, eggs, and milk.
4. Gradually add the dry ingredients to the wet ingredients mixture while stirring until just combined.
5. Fold in the shredded cheddar, chopped spring onions, and crumbled bacon.
6. Divide the batter equally among the muffin cups, filling them about two-thirds full.
7. Bake for 20 minutes, or until the muffins are golden brown and a toothpick inserted into the center comes out clean.
8. Allow the muffins to cool in the tin on a wire rack for 5 minutes, then remove from the tin to cool completely.
9. Serve these savory sourdough muffins warm. They can be enjoyed as a breakfast treat, snack, or as a compliment to a meal. Enjoy!

SOFT PRETZEL BITES

Preparation time: 90 minutes
Cooking time: 15 minutes
Servings: 4

INGREDIENTS:

- 1/2 cup of your sourdough starter discard
- 1 1/2 cups warm water (110 to 115 degrees F)
- 4 cups all-purpose flour
- 2 teaspoons salt
- 1 tablespoon brown sugar
- 1 teaspoon active dry yeast
- 6 cups of water for boiling
- 1/4 cup baking soda for boiling
- Coarse sea salt for sprinkling on top

INSTRUCTIONS:

1. In a large bowl, combine your sourdough starter discard, warm water, flour, salt, brown sugar, and active dry yeast.
2. Mix until it forms a sticky dough.
3. Turn the dough out onto a floured surface and knead until it becomes smooth and elastic, about 8-10 minutes.
4. Place the kneaded dough in a greased bowl, cover and let it rise for about an hour or until it doubles in size.
5. Once the dough has risen, preheat your oven to 425 degrees F and line a baking sheet with parchment paper.

6. Bring the 6 cups of water and the baking soda to a rolling boil in an 8-quart saucepan or roasting pan
7. While the water boils, divide the dough into 4 pieces. Roll out each piece into a long rope and cut into bite-sized pieces.
8. Boil the pretzel pieces in the baking soda water for 30 seconds each, making sure not to overcrowd the pan.
9. Remove with a slotted spoon and place on your prepared baking sheet. Sprinkle with the coarse sea salt.
10. Bake for 12-15 minutes or until the pretzel bites are golden brown.
11. Allow to cool for a few minutes before serving. Enjoy as is, or with your favorite mustard or cheese dipping sauce.

SPINACH DIP BREAD BOWL

Preparation time: 20 minutes
Cooking time: 25 minutes
Servings: 4

INGREDIENTS:
For the Sourdough Discard Bread Bowl:
- 1 large round Sourdough bread (about 1 lb)
- 1 cup Sourdough discard
- 2 tablespoons olive oil

For the Spinach Dip:
- 1 cup frozen chopped spinach, thawed and drained
- 1 cup sour cream
- 1 cup cream cheese, softened
- 1 cup grated Monterey Jack cheese
- 1 cup grated Parmesan cheese
- 1 medium onion, finely chopped
- 2 cloves garlic, minced
- Salt and black pepper to taste

INSTRUCTIONS:
1. Preheat your oven to 350°F (175°C).
2. Cut a large circle on top of the sourdough bread and gently remove the bread inside creating a bowl. Make sure not to cut through the bottom.
3. Brush the inside of the bread bowl and the removed bread top with the sourdough discard and olive oil mixture.
4. Place your bread bowl and top on a baking sheet lined with parchment paper and bake in the preheated oven for 15 minutes, or until they become crispy. Set aside.
5. For the spinach dip, combine the spinach, sour cream, cream cheese, Monterey Jack and Parmesan cheese, onion, garlic, salt, and pepper in a large bowl. Mix well until the ingredients are thoroughly combined.
6. Spoon the spinach mixture into the sourdough bread bowl, filling it to the brim.
7. Return the filled bread bowl to the oven and bake for an additional 10 minutes, or until the cheese is melted and bubbly.

8. Carefully remove the bread bowl from the oven and let it cool for a few minutes before serving.

VEGGIE TART

Preparation time: 30 minutes
Cooking time: 45 minutes
Servings: 4

INGREDIENTS:
For the Sourdough Crust:
- 1 cup of sourdough discard
- 1 cup of all-purpose flour
- 1/2 cup of cold butter, cut into cubes
- 1/2 teaspoon of salt
- 1/4 cup of ice water

For the Filling:
- 2 cups of seasonal vegetables (zucchini, tomatoes, bell peppers, etc.), thinly sliced
- 1 cup of grated cheddar cheese
- 1 cup of full-fat milk
- 2 medium eggs
- Salt and pepper to taste
- A handful of fresh herbs (basil, thyme, rosemary), chopped

INSTRUCTIONS:
1. Start with the sourdough crust. In a large bowl, combine the sourdough discard, flour, and salt.
2. Add the cubed cold butter to the mixture and use your fingers to mix it in until the texture resembles coarse breadcrumbs.
3. Gradually pour in the ice water, kneading the dough until it comes together. If the dough is still too dry, add a bit more water.
4. Roll the dough out to fit a 9-inch tart pan. Press it into the pan and trim any excess dough. Place the pan in the fridge to chill for about 20 minutes.
5. Preheat your oven to 375°F (190°C).
6. To make the filling, beat the eggs in a large bowl. Add in the milk, cheese, salt, pepper, and chopped fresh herbs.
7. Take the tart pan out of the fridge and arrange the sliced vegetables on top of the sourdough crust. Pour the egg mixture over the vegetables.
8. Bake the tart for about 45 minutes, or until the crust is golden and the filling is set.
9. Allow the tart to cool for a few minutes before serving. Enjoy your Sourdough Discard Veggie Tart!

MAIN DISHES

BURRITO BOWLS

Preparation time: 45 minutes
Cooking time: 20 minutes
Servings: 4

INGREDIENTS:
For the flatbread:
- 1/2 cup sourdough discard
- 2 cups all-purpose flour
- 1/2 cup water
- 1/2 teaspoon salt
- 1 tablespoon olive oil

For the burrito bowl:
- 1 cup cooked rice
- 1 can black beans, drained and rinsed, or 1 cup cooked black beans
- 1 cup corn
- 1 cup shredded lettuce
- 1 cup diced tomatoes
- 1 cup shredded cheddar cheese
- 1/2 cup diced red onion
- 1/2 cup diced avocado
- 1/2 cup salsa
- 1/4 cup sour cream or Greek yogurt

INSTRUCTIONS:
1. In a large bowl, combine the flour, sourdough discard, water, and salt. Stir until it forms a sticky dough.
2. Turn the dough onto a floured surface and knead until it becomes elastic.
3. Divide the dough into four pieces and roll each piece into a thin, round flatbread.
4. Heat a large skillet over medium heat and add olive oil. Once the skillet is hot, add a flatbread and cook for 2-3 minutes each side or until lightly browned. Repeat with remaining flatbreads.
5. To make the burrito bowls, divide the cooked rice between four bowls.
6. Top each bowl evenly with black beans, corn, diced tomatoes, shredded lettuce, shredded cheese, diced onion, and diced avocado.
7. Add a dollop of salsa and sour cream on top of each bowl.
8. Use a piece of the sourdough discard flatbread to scoop up the ingredients in the bowl or break it into pieces and sprinkle it on top.

CALZONES

Preparation time: 2 hours (including dough rising time)
Cooking time: 15 minutes
Servings: 4

INGREDIENTS:
For the sourdough discard dough:
- 1 cup of sourdough starter discard
- 1/2 cup of warm water
- 2 1/2 cups of bread flour, plus extra for kneading
- 1 teaspoon of salt
- 1 teaspoon of sugar
- 1 tablespoon of olive oil

For the filling:

- 1 1/2 cups of shredded mozzarella cheese
- 1/2 cup of pizza sauce
- 1 cup of your favorite pizza toppings (such as pepperoni, cooked sausage, diced bell peppers, sliced olives, etc.)
- 1 egg (for egg wash)

INSTRUCTIONS:
1. In a large mixing bowl, combine the sourdough discard, warm water, bread flour, salt, sugar, and olive oil. Mix until a soft dough forms.
2. Turn the dough out onto a lightly floured surface and knead for 5 to 10 minutes, until the dough is smooth and elastic.
3. Place the dough in a greased bowl, cover, and let rise in a warm place for about 1 hour, or until the dough has doubled in size.
4. Preheat your oven to 475 degrees F. Divide the dough into 4 equal pieces and roll each piece into a circle about 1/4 inch thick.
5. Spoon pizza sauce onto half of each dough circle, leaving a border around the edge. Add your favorite pizza toppings and sprinkle generously with shredded mozzarella cheese.
6. Fold the dough over the filling to create a half-circle and crimp the edges to seal.
7. Beat the egg with a little water to make an egg wash and brush it over the top of each calzone.
8. Bake for 15 minutes, or until the calzones are golden brown.
9. Allow to cool for a few minutes before slicing and serving.

BBQ CHICKEN FLATBREAD

Preparation time: 30 minutes
Cooking time: 15 minutes
Servings: 4

INGREDIENTS:
For the Flatbread:
- 1 cup Sourdough Discard
- 1 cup All-purpose flour
- 1/4 cup Olive oil
- 1 tsp Salt

For the Toppings:
- 1 cup BBQ sauce
- 2 cups shredded cooked Chicken Breasts
- 1 cup sliced Red Onions
- 2 cups shredded Mozzarella Cheese
- 1/4 cup chopped fresh Cilantro

INSTRUCTIONS:
1. Preheat your oven to 450 degrees F. If you have a pizza stone, place it in the oven while it preheats.
2. In a large bowl, combine your sourdough discard, flour, olive oil, and salt. Mix until a sticky dough forms. Turn the dough out onto a lightly floured surface and knead

for about 5 minutes or until smooth.

3. Divide your dough into 4 equal parts. Roll each piece into a circle about 1/4 inch thick.

4. If you have a pizza stone, carefully remove it from the oven and place one of your flatbreads on it. If you don't have a pizza stone, place your flatbread on a baking sheet.

5. Spread about a 1/4 cup of BBQ sauce onto your flatbread, leaving a small border around the edges for the crust. Top with about a 1/2 cup of shredded chicken, a 1/4 cup of sliced onions, and a 1/2 cup of mozzarella cheese.

6. Bake in the preheated oven for 12-15 minutes, or until the cheese is bubbly and the crust is golden.

7. Repeat with the remaining flatbreads.

8. Once the flatbreads are done baking, sprinkle with chopped cilantro.

9. Serve and enjoy your homemade BBQ Chicken Flatbread! They are delicious served hot out of the oven.

CHICKEN POT PIE

Preparation time: 60 minutes
Cooking time: 50 minutes
Servings: 4

INGREDIENTS:

For the filling:
- 2 cups chopped cooked chicken
- 2 cups mixed vegetables (like carrots, peas, and celery)
- 1 cup diced onion
- 2 cloves garlic, minced
- 3 cups chicken broth
- ¼ cup all-purpose flour
- 2 tablespoons butter
- Salt and pepper to taste

For the sourdough crust:
- 1 cup sourdough discard
- 1 and ½ cups all-purpose flour
- ½ cup unsalted butter, chilled and cut into cubes
- ½ teaspoon salt
- 1 tablespoon sugar
- 4-6 tablespoons ice water

INSTRUCTIONS:
For the filling:

1. In a large pot, melt the butter over medium heat. Add the onions, and sauté until onions are translucent for about 4-5 minutes.

2. Stir in the garlic, and sauté until fragrant for about 1 minute. Then, add the flour, stirring it in until no dry spots remain.

3. Slowly pour in the chicken broth, stirring continuously. Mix in the chopped chicken and vegetables and bring the mixture to a simmer. Let it cook until the mixture has thickened, about 10 minutes. Season with salt and pepper.

4. Transfer the filling to a pie dish, then set aside to cool slightly.

For the sourdough crust:
1. In a large bowl, stir together the flour, salt, and sugar. Cut in the butter until the mixture resembles coarse crumbs.
2. Stir in the sourdough discard, then add ice water one tablespoon at a time, mixing until a dough forms.
3. Turn the dough out onto a floured surface and knead it a few times to bring it together. Roll the dough out into a circle that's big enough to cover your pie dish.
4. Preheat your oven to 375°F (190°C).
5. Lay the crust over the cooled filling in the pie dish, crimping the edges to seal. Cut a few slits in the top of the crust to allow steam to escape.
6. Bake in the preheated oven for 30-35 minutes, or until the crust is golden and the filling is bubbling.

ENCHILADAS

Preparation time: 30 minutes
Cooking time: 20 minutes
Servings: 4

INGREDIENTS:
- 1 cup of sourdough discard
- 1 cup of all-purpose flour
- 1/2 teaspoon of salt
- 3-4 tablespoons of olive oil
- 2 cups of enchilada sauce
- 1 1/2 cups of shredded chicken
- 1 cup of shredded cheddar cheese
- 1/2 cup of diced onions
- 1/2 cup of sliced olives
- 1 green bell pepper, diced
- 1/2 cup of sour cream
- Fresh cilantro for garnish

INSTRUCTIONS:
1. In a large mixing bowl, combine the sourdough discard, flour, and salt. Slowly add the olive oil, continue mixing until a soft dough forms.
2. Divide the dough into 8 equal pieces and roll out each piece into a thin, round tortilla.
3. Preheat your oven to 375°F (190°C).
4. Heat a skillet over medium heat and lightly cook each tortilla for about 2 minutes on each side. Set aside.
5. In the same skillet, add a little more oil, if necessary, then sauté the onions and bell peppers until they're softened.
6. Assemble the enchiladas by placing a scoop of shredded chicken, a spoonful of the onion and bell pepper mixture, and a sprinkle of cheese on each tortilla. Roll them up tightly and place them in a baking dish.
7. Pour the enchilada sauce over the rolled tortillas in the baking dish, then sprinkle with the

remaining cheese and sliced olives.

8. Bake for about 20 minutes, or until the cheese is melted and bubbly.

9. Serve your Sourdough Discard Enchiladas warm with a dollop of sour cream and a sprinkle of fresh cilantro on top. Enjoy this tangy twist on a Mexican favorite!

FISH TACOS

Preparation time: 20 minutes
Cooking time: 15 minutes
Servings: 4

INGREDIENTS:
For the Fish:
- 1 lb. white fish fillets (like cod, haddock, or tilapia)
- 1 cup sourdough discard
- 1/2 cup all-purpose flour
- 1/2 cup cornmeal
- 1/2 teaspoon baking powder
- 1/2 teaspoon salt
- 1/2 teaspoon black pepper
- 1 cup vegetable oil for frying

For the Tacos:
- 8 small corn tortillas
- 2 cups shredded lettuce
- 1 cup diced tomatoes
- 1/2 cup diced onions
- 1 diced green pepper
- 1/2 cup cilantro leaves
- 1/2 cup crema or sour cream
- Lime wedges, to serve

INSTRUCTIONS:

1. Rinse the fish fillets, pat them dry and cut into 1-inch-wide strips.

2. In a shallow bowl, whisk together the sourdough discard, flour, cornmeal, baking powder, salt, and pepper to form the batter.

3. Dip each piece of fish into the batter, ensuring it's fully coated.

4. In a large frying pan, heat the vegetable oil over medium-high heat.

5. Fry the battered fish in the heated oil, turning occasionally, until they're golden brown and crispy, about 5-7 minutes. Make sure not to overcrowd the pan, fry in batches if necessary.

6. Drain the fried fish on kitchen paper to remove any excess oil.

7. Warm up the corn tortillas over an open flame or in a dry hot pan until they're soft and pliable.

8. To assemble the tacos, place a base of shredded lettuce on each tortilla, followed by the crispy fish.

9. Top with the diced tomatoes, onions, green peppers, and a sprinkle of cilantro.

10. Drizzle with crema or sour cream, serve with lime wedges on the side for squeezing over the top.

11. Enjoy these tangy and crunchy sourdough discard fish tacos. Enjoy the added depth of flavor and texture the sourdough discard adds to your taco night.

GNOCCHI

Preparation time: 30 minutes
Cooking time: 15 minutes
Servings: 4

INGREDIENTS:
- 1 cup of sourdough discard
- 1 large egg
- 1.5 2 cups all-purpose flour, plus more for dusting
- 1 teaspoon of salt
- 1/2 teaspoon of ground black pepper
- 4 tablespoons of unsalted butter
- 2 cloves crushed garlic
- 2 teaspoons of fresh chopped sage

INSTRUCTIONS:
1. Start by beating the egg in a large bowl. Add your sourdough discard to the beaten egg and mix well until you achieve a smooth consistency.
2. Slowly add the flour to your egg and discard mixture, stirring continuously. You're aiming to achieve a soft, slightly sticky dough. Depending on the hydration of your discard, you might need more or less flour.
3. On a floured surface, knead your dough gently for about 2-3 minutes until smooth and pliable.
4. Divide your dough into 4 equal parts. Roll each part into a long rope, about 1/2 inch in diameter. Cut the rope into 1-inch-long pieces to form your gnocchi.
5. Bring a large pot of salted water to the boil. Add your gnocchi and cook for about 3-4 minutes. They will float to the top when cooked.
6. While your gnocchi are boiling, melt the butter in a large skillet over medium heat. Add the crushed garlic and sage and let it sizzle for a minute or two, taking care not to let the garlic burn.
7. Using a slotted spoon, transfer the cooked gnocchi directly to the skillet with the garlic and sage butter. Sauté for a minute or two until they're nicely coated in the butter and just beginning to color.
8. Season with salt and black pepper to taste. Serve your sourdough discard gnocchi hot, with a little grated Parmesan on top if desired. Enjoy your tangy twist on the classic gnocchi.

NOODLES

Preparation time: 35 minutes
Cooking time: 5 minutes
Servings: 4 people

INGREDIENTS:
1/2 cup of sourdough discard
2 Large eggs
3-4 cups of all-purpose flour
1 teaspoon of salt
Water (as needed)

INSTRUCTIONS:
1. In a large mixing bowl, combine your sourdough discard and eggs. Mix these ingredients

together until they are thoroughly combined.

2. Slowly begin to incorporate the flour into your egg and discard mixture. You'll want to incorporate the flour slowly to prevent any lumps from forming in your noodle dough.
3. Once all your flour has been incorporated, add in your salt, and continue to stir your dough. If the dough seems too dry, gradually add some water until it's pliable and not sticking to the sides of the bowl.
4. Knead your dough on a floured surface for about 5-10 minutes, or until it becomes elastic and smooth. Wrap the dough in plastic wrap and let it rest for 20 minutes.
5. After the dough has rested, roll it out into a thin sheet using a rolling pin. Once the dough is rolled out, cut it into long, thin strips using a sharp knife or a pasta cutting tool.
6. Bring a pot of salted water to a boil. Once the water is boiling, carefully add your noodles and cook them for about 5-7 minutes, or until they are al dente.
7. Strain your noodles and serve them hot with your sauce or toppings of choice. Enjoy your homemade sourdough discard noodles!

PIEROGI

Preparation time: 180 minutes
Cooking time: 30 minutes
Servings: 4

INGREDIENTS:
For the dough:
- 1 cup of active sourdough starter discard
- 3 cups all-purpose flour
- 1/2 cup water
- 1 teaspoon salt
- 1 egg

For the filling:
- 2 large russet potatoes
- 1 cup grated sharp cheddar cheese
- Salt and pepper, to taste
- 1/2 cup finely chopped onions

For serving:
- Melted butter
- Sour cream
- Chopped fresh chives

INSTRUCTIONS:
1. Make the dough: In a large bowl, combine the sourdough starter discard, flour, water, salt, and egg. Mix until you have a smooth and elastic dough. Cover with a damp cloth and let rest for 2 hours.
2. Prepare the filling: While the dough is resting, peel, chop, and boil the potatoes until they are soft. Drain them and return to the pot. Add the cheddar cheese,

salt, pepper, and onions. Mash until smooth.

3. Roll out the dough on a floured surface to about 1/8 inch thick. Cut out circles using a biscuit cutter or glass.
4. Spoon a small amount of potato filling into the center of each dough circle. Fold the dough over the filling and pinch the edges to seal.
5. Boil a large pot of salted water. Add the pierogi and cook until they rise to the top, about 5 minutes. Drain.
6. To serve, fry the pierogi in some melted butter until golden brown. Serve hot with sour cream and a sprinkle of fresh chives. Enjoy your homemade Sourdough Discard Pierogi.

QUESADILLAS

Preparation time: 30 minutes
Cooking time: 15 minutes
Servings: 4

INGREDIENTS:
For the tortillas:
- 2 1/2 cups of all-purpose flour
- 1/2 cup of sourdough discard
- 1 teaspoon of salt
- 1/2 cup of water
- 3 tablespoons of vegetable oil

For the filling:
- 8 ounces of shredded cheese (your choice: cheddar, Monterey jack, etc.)

- 1 large bell pepper, diced
- 1 large onion, diced
- 1 cup of cooked chicken, diced
- 1/2 cup of chopped fresh cilantro
- salt and pepper to taste
- Additional vegetable oil for cooking

INSTRUCTIONS:
1. Begin with the tortillas. In a large bowl, mix together the flour, sourdough discard and salt. Stir in the water and vegetable oil until a dough forms.
2. Knead the dough for a few minutes, until it becomes smooth. Divide the dough into 8 equal parts and roll each piece into a ball. Let the dough rest for about 15 minutes.
3. While the dough is resting, prepare your filling. In a large skillet, sauté the diced bell pepper and onion with a splash of vegetable oil until they become soft. Stir in the cooked chicken and season the mixture with salt and pepper. Set the filling aside.
4. Roll out each dough ball into a circle, about 8 inches in diameter.
5. Heat a large skillet over medium heat and brush with vegetable oil. Place a tortilla on the skillet, spoon some of the chicken and vegetable mixture on one half of the tortilla, and sprinkle with shredded cheese and a bit of the chopped cilantro.
6. Fold the tortilla in half, covering the filling. Cook for about 1-2

minutes on each side, or until the quesadilla is golden brown and the cheese has melted. Repeat with the remaining tortillas and filling.

7. Serve your Sourdough Discard Quesadillas hot, with your favorite salsa or sour cream. Enjoy these tangy and savory quesadillas that have a unique twist!

RAVIOLI

Preparation time: 90 minutes
Cooking time: 10 minutes
Servings: 4

INGREDIENTS:
For the Pasta:
- 1 1/2 cups all-purpose flour
- 1/2 cup sourdough discard
- 1/2 teaspoon salt
- 2 large eggs

For the Filling:
- 1 cup ricotta cheese
- 1/2 cup grated Parmesan cheese
- 1 large egg
- 1 tablespoon fresh minced parsley
- 1/2 teaspoon dried basil
- salt and pepper to taste

For the Sauce (optional):
- 1/4 cup butter
- 1 clove garlic, minced
- 1/4 cup fresh minced parsley

INSTRUCTIONS:

1. Start by making the pasta. In a large mixing bowl, combine the flour and salt. Create a well in the center and add the sourdough discard and eggs.

2. Using a fork, gradually incorporate the flour into the wet ingredients until a sticky dough forms.

3. Knead the dough for about 10 minutes, or until it becomes smooth and elastic. Cover the dough and let it rest for at least 30 minutes.

4. While the dough is resting, prepare the filling. In a separate bowl, combine the ricotta cheese, Parmesan cheese, egg, parsley, basil, salt, and pepper.

5. After the dough has rested, roll it out into a thin sheet. Place dollops of the cheese mixture onto one half of the pasta sheet, leaving about 2 inches between each dollop.

6. Fold the other half of the pasta sheet over the dollops of cheese and press around each one to seal it, cutting out the ravioli using a circular cutter or knife.

7. Bring a large pot of salted water to a boil. Add the ravioli and cook for about 3-4 minutes or until they float to the top.

8. If desired, you can prepare a simple sauce while the ravioli boil. Heat the butter in a pan over medium heat. Add the minced garlic and cook until fragrant. Stir

in the fresh parsley and remove from heat.

9. Drain the ravioli and serve with the prepared sauce, or with your sauce of choice.

STROMBOLI

Preparation time: 60 minutes
Cooking time: 25 minutes
Servings: 4

INGREDIENTS:
- 1 batch of pizza dough (store bought or homemade)
- 1 cup sourdough discard
- 1 cup shredded mozzarella cheese
- 1/2 cup grated Parmesan cheese
- 1/2 cup sliced salami
- 1/2 cup sliced pepperoni
- 1/2 cup sliced bell pepper
- 1/2 cup sliced onion
- 1 tablespoon olive oil
- 1/2 teaspoon garlic powder
- 11/2 teaspoon dried oregano
- 11/2 teaspoon dried basil
- 1Salt and pepper to taste
- 11 egg (for egg wash)
- 11 tablespoon water (for egg wash)

INSTRUCTIONS:
1. Preheat your oven to 400 degrees Fahrenheit.
2. While the oven is heating, roll out your pizza dough into a 1/4-inch-thick rectangle on a floured surface.

3. Spread the sourdough discard evenly over the pizza dough, leaving a 1-inch margin on all sides. This will enhance the flavor of the stromboli and help maintain a moist interior.
4. Layer the cheeses, salami, pepperoni, bell pepper, and onion over the sourdough discard.
5. Sprinkle the garlic powder, oregano, basil, salt, and pepper evenly over the filled dough.
6. Roll up the dough tightly from one of the long sides, making sure to tuck in any fillings that try to escape.
7. Once rolled, place the stromboli seam side down on a parchment lined baking sheet.
8. Beat together the egg and water to make an egg wash and brush this over the stromboli.
9. Bake in the preheated oven for 20-25 minutes, or until the stromboli is golden brown and crispy on the outside.
10. Allow the stromboli to cool for 5-10 minutes before slicing and serving.

VEGGIE BURGERS

Preparation time: 30 minutes
Cooking time: 20 minutes
Servings: 4

INGREDIENTS:
- 1 cup of sourdough discard
- 1 1/2 cups of cooked quinoa

- 2 cups of mixed vegetables (e.g., bell peppers, zucchini, carrots), finely chopped
- 1 large egg
- 1/2 cup of breadcrumbs
- 1/2 cup of grated cheddar cheese
- 2 tablespoons of soy sauce
- 1/2 teaspoon of garlic powder
- 1/2 teaspoon of onion powder
- Salt and pepper to taste
- Vegetable oil for frying
- 4 hamburger buns
- Toppings: lettuce, tomato slices, pickles, onions, avocado etc.

INSTRUCTIONS:
1. In a large bowl, combine the sourdough discard, quinoa, mixed vegetables, egg, breadcrumbs, cheddar cheese, soy sauce, garlic powder, onion powder, salt, and pepper. Mix until the ingredients are well combined.
2. Divide the mixture into 4 equal parts and shape each part into a burger patty.
3. Heat the vegetable oil in a large skillet over medium heat. Carefully add the patties to the skillet, and cook until browned and crispy, about 5-7 minutes on each side. Ensure that the patties are cooked evenly and thoroughly.
4. Serve the veggie burgers on buns with your preferred toppings like lettuce, tomato slices, pickles, onions, avocado etc.
5. Enjoy your flavorful sourdough discard veggie burgers!

DESSERTS

APPLE FRITTERS

Preparation time: 15 minutes
Cooking time: 15 minutes
Servings: 4

INGREDIENTS:
- 1 cup of sourdough starter discard
- 2 large apples, peeled and diced
- 1 cup of all-purpose flour
- 1/4 cup of sugar
- 1 large egg
- 1/2 teaspoon of cinnamon
- 1/4 teaspoon of nutmeg
- 1/2 teaspoon of vanilla extract
- 1/2 teaspoon of salt
- 1 teaspoon of baking powder
- Vegetable oil for frying
- Powdered sugar for dusting

INSTRUCTIONS:
1. In a large mixing bowl, combine the sourdough discard, flour, sugar, egg, cinnamon, nutmeg, vanilla extract, salt, and baking powder. Stir until well combined.
2. Add the diced apples to the mixture and gently stir until all apple pieces are well-coated.
3. In a heavy-bottomed pot or deep fryer, heat the vegetable oil over medium high heat. The oil should be about 2 inches deep in the pot.
4. Use a cookie scoop or tablespoon to drop spoonsful of the apple batter into the hot oil. Be careful not to crowd the pot.
5. Fry the fritters for 2-3 minutes on each side, or until they become a lovely golden-brown color.
6. Using a slotted spoon, carefully remove the fritters from the oil and let them drain on paper towels.
7. Dust the fritters with powdered sugar while they are still warm.
8. Serve your sourdough discard apple fritters warm and enjoy their tangy, sweet flavor.

APPLE PIE

Preparation time: 40 minutes
Cooking time: 50 minutes
Servings: 4

INGREDIENTS:
For the crust:
- 2 cups of sourdough discard
- 2 1/2 cups all-purpose flour
- 1 tablespoon granulated sugar
- 1 teaspoon salt
- 1 cup unsalted butter, cold and cut into small pieces
- 1/4 1/2 cup ice water

For the filling:
- 6 medium apples, peeled and sliced
- 1/2 cup granulated sugar
- 1/4 cup all-purpose flour
- 2 teaspoons ground cinnamon
- 1/4 teaspoon nutmeg
- 1/4 teaspoon salt
- 1 teaspoon vanilla extract

For the topping:

- 1/4 cup heavy cream
- 1 tablespoon granulated sugar

INSTRUCTIONS:

1. For the crust, in a large bowl combine the sourdough discard, flour, sugar, and salt. Add the butter and use your hands or a pastry cutter to cut it into the dry ingredients until a crumbly dough starts to form.
2. Gradually add the ice water, starting with 1/4 cup, and mix until the dough comes together. Be careful to not overwork it.
3. Wrap the dough in plastic wrap and refrigerate for at least 30 minutes.
4. After the dough has chilled, roll it out on a floured surface to fit your pie dish. Gently press it into the dish and trim any excess, leaving a small overhang.
5. For the filling, in a large bowl combine the apples, sugar, flour, cinnamon, nutmeg, salt, and vanilla. Mix until the apples are evenly coated.
6. Pour the filling into your prepared pie crust.
7. Roll out the remaining dough and cut into strips or shapes as desired to create a lattice or full top crust.
8. Brush the top of the pie with the heavy cream and sprinkle with sugar.
9. Preheat your oven to 375°F (190°C) and bake the pie for about 50 minutes, or until the crust is golden and the filling is bubbling. If the crust starts to get too brown, you can cover it with foil.
10. Allow the pie to cool before serving to allow the filling to set.

BANANA CREAM PIE

Preparation time: 45 minutes
Cooking time: 20 minutes
Servings: 4

INGREDIENTS:
For the crust:
- 1 1/2 cups of all-purpose flour
- 1/2 cup of sourdough discard
- 1/4 cup of granulated sugar
- 1/4 teaspoon of salt
- 1/2 cup of unsalted butter, cold and cut into pieces

For the filling:
- 1/2 cup of granulated sugar
- 1/4 cup of cornstarch
- 1/4 teaspoon of salt
- 3 large egg yolks
- 1 1/2 cups of milk
- 1/2 cup of heavy cream
- 2 ripe bananas, mashed
- 1 teaspoon of pure vanilla extract

For the topping:
- 1 cup of heavy cream
- 2 tablespoons of powdered sugar
- 1/2 teaspoon of pure vanilla extract

INSTRUCTIONS:

1. Begin with mixing the flour, discard, sugar, and salt in bowl of a food processor.
2. Add the cold butter and pulse until the mixture resembles coarse crumbs.
3. Press the crust mixture into a pie dish and chill for at least 30 minutes.
4. Preheat the oven to 350°F (180°C). Bake crust for 20 minutes or until golden brown. Cool completely on a wire rack.
5. In a medium saucepan, combine sugar, cornstarch, salt, egg yolks, milk, and heavy cream. Cook over medium heat, stirring constantly, until mixture comes to a boil.
6. Continue to cook while stirring for another minute, then remove from heat.
7. Stir in the mashed bananas and vanilla. Pour the filling into the cooled pie crust.
8. Cover with plastic wrap and chill for at least 4 hours, or until set.
9. Before serving, make the topping by whipping together heavy cream, powdered sugar, and vanilla until soft peaks form.
10. Top the pie with cream and serve chilled. Enjoy your Sourdough Discard Banana Cream Pie!

BISCOTTI

Preparation time: 15 minutes
Cooking time: 45 minutes
Servings: 4

INGREDIENTS:
- 1 cup of sourdough starter discard
- 1/2 cup of unsalted butter, softened
- 3/4 cup of granulated sugar
- 2 large eggs
- 2 teaspoons of vanilla extract
- 3 cups of all-purpose flour
- 1.5 teaspoons of baking powder
- 1/2 teaspoon of salt
- 1 cup of chopped almonds

INSTRUCTIONS:
1. Preheat your oven to 350°F (180°C) and line a baking sheet with parchment paper.
2. In a large bowl, cream together the butter and sugar until light and fluffy.
3. Beat in the eggs one at a time, followed by vanilla extract and sourdough starter discard.
4. In a separate bowl, mix together the all-purpose flour, baking powder, and salt.
5. Slowly add the dry ingredients into the wet ingredients, mixing until combined.
6. Fold in the chopped almonds.
7. Divide the dough in half and form two logs on the prepared baking sheet.
8. Bake for 25 minutes until the logs are set and lightly browned.
9. Remove from the oven and let cool for 15 minutes.

10. Slice the logs into 1/2-inch-thick biscotti and lay flat on the baking sheet.
11. Bake for an additional 10-20 minutes, or until the biscotti are crisp and golden brown.
12. Let the biscotti cool before serving, they are best served with a cup of coffee for dipping.

BLUEBERRY BUCKLE

Preparation time: 20 minutes
Cooking time: 50 minutes
Servings: 4

INGREDIENTS:
For the Sourdough Discard Crumble:
- 1 cup of Sourdough Discard
- 1/2 cup of All-Purpose Flour
- 1/4 cup of Brown Sugar
- 1/4 cup of Unsalted Butter, Cold and Cubed
- 1/2 teaspoon of Ground Cinnamon

For the Blueberry Buckle:
- 2 cups Fresh Blueberries
- 1 cup of Granulated Sugar
- 1/2 cup of Unsalted Butter, at Room Temperature
- 1 large Egg
- 1 teaspoon of Vanilla Extract
- 1 cup of All-Purpose Flour
- 1/2 teaspoon Baking Powder
- 1/4 teaspoon of Salt

INSTRUCTIONS:
1. First, mix all the ingredients for the sourdough discard crumble in a bowl. Use your fingers to combine everything together until it forms a loose crumble texture. Set aside.
2. Preheat your oven to 375°F (190°C). Butter a 9-inch pie dish and set aside.
3. In a large bowl, beat together the sugar and butter for the buckle until creamy. Add the egg and vanilla extract and continue to beat until well combined.
4. In another bowl, whisk together the flour, baking powder, and salt. Gradually add the flour mixture to the sugar and butter mixture and mix until fully combined.
5. Fold in the fresh blueberries gently so not to burst them.
6. Transfer the buckle mixture into the prepared pie dish.
7. Then, evenly distribute the sourdough discard crumble over the top of the batter in the pie dish.
8. Bake for 50 minutes, or until a toothpick inserted into the center of the buckle comes out clean.
9. Allow the buckle to cool for 10 minutes before slicing and serving. Enjoy your unique Sourdough Discard Blueberry Buckle!

BOSTON CREAM PIE

Preparation time: 30 minutes
Cooking time: 25 minutes
Servings: 4

INGREDIENTS:

For the Sourdough Cake:
- 1/2 cup unsalted butter, room temperature
- 1 cup sugar
- 2 large eggs
- 1 teaspoon vanilla extract
- 2 cups all-purpose flour
- 2 teaspoons baking powder
- 1/2 teaspoon salt
- 1 cup sourdough discard
- 1/2 cup milk

For the Custard Filling:
- 2 cups whole milk
- 1/2 cup sugar
- 1/4 cup cornstarch
- 1/8 teaspoon salt
- 4 large egg yolks
- 2 tablespoons unsalted butter
- 1 teaspoon vanilla extract

For the Chocolate Glaze:
- 4 ounces semi-sweet chocolate, chopped
- 1/4 cup unsalted butter
- 1 tablespoon corn syrup

INSTRUCTIONS:
1. Preheat your oven to 350°F. Grease and flour two 8-inch cake pans.
2. In a mixing bowl, cream together the butter and sugar until light and fluffy. Add the eggs and vanilla and continue to mix until well combined.
3. In a separate bowl, combine the flour, baking powder, and salt. Gradually add this to the butter mixture, alternating with the sourdough discard and milk. Start and finish with the dry mixture. Mix until smooth.
4. Pour the batter into the prepared cake pans, smoothing out the tops. Bake for 25 minutes, or until a toothpick inserted into the center of the cakes comes out clean.
5. While the cakes are baking, prepare the custard filling. In a medium saucepan, combine milk, sugar, cornstarch, and salt. Bring to a simmer over medium heat, continually stirring.
6. Whip egg yolks in a separate bowl. Gradually pour a bit of the hot milk mixture into the yolks, stirring constantly to avoid cooking the eggs. Pour the yolk mixture back to the saucepan and cook for 2 minutes at a simmer, stirring constantly.
7. Remove pan from heat. Stir in butter and vanilla until combined. Let it cool, cover with cling wrap directly on custard surface to avoid a skin layer forming.
8. Once cakes are baked and cooled, and custard is chilled, spread the custard over the bottom layer of the cake, then top with the second cake layer.
9. Melt the chocolate, butter, and corn syrup together for the glaze in a double boiler or in short

bursts in a microwave. Stir until smooth, then pour over assembled cake.

10. Refrigerate the cake until set, approximately 2 hours, before serving. Enjoy a tangy spin on a classic dessert with your Sourdough Discard Boston Cream Pie!

BROWNIES

Preparation time: 15 minutes
Cooking time: 30 minutes
Servings: 4

INGREDIENTS:
- 1 cup of all-purpose flour
- 1/4 cup of unsweetened cocoa powder
- 1 teaspoon of salt
- 1/2 cup (or 1 stick) of unsalted butter
- 1 cup of granulated sugar
- 2 large eggs
- 1 teaspoon of pure vanilla extract
- 1 cup of semi-sweet chocolate chips
- 1 cup of sourdough discard

INSTRUCTIONS:
1. Preheat your oven to 350 degrees Fahrenheit (175 degrees Celsius). Line an 8-inch square baking pan with parchment paper, leaving an overhang on two sides to lift the finished brownies out.

2. In a medium bowl, whisk together the flour, cocoa powder, and salt. Set aside.

3. In a microwave-safe bowl, melt the butter in the microwave. Add the sugar, stirring to combine. Allow the mixture to cool a bit before proceeding.

4. Stir in the eggs and vanilla extract to the butter/sugar mixture, one at a time, mixing well after each addition.

5. Slowly whisk in the flour mixture until well combined.

6. Gently fold in the sourdough discard and chocolate chips, stirring just until combined.

7. Transfer the brownie batter into the prepared baking pan, spreading it evenly with a spatula.

8. Bake for 25-30 minutes, or until a toothpick inserted in the center comes out with a few moist crumbs.

9. Allow the brownies to cool in the pan on a wire rack for at least 10 minutes before lifting out the parchment paper and cutting them into squares.

10. Enjoy your Sourdough Discard Brownies warm or at room temperature.

CARROT CAKE

Preparation time: 30 minutes
Cooking time: 35 minutes
Servings: 4

INGREDIENTS:

For the carrot cake:
- 2 cups of all-purpose flour
- 1 cup of sourdough discard
- 1 cup of granulated sugar
- 3/4 cup of vegetable oil
- 2 tsp of baking soda
- 1/2 tsp of salt
- 1 tsp of cinnamon
- 1/2 tsp of nutmeg
- 2 eggs
- 1 1/2 cups of finely grated carrots

For the cream cheese frosting:
- 4 ounces of cream cheese, softened
- 2 cups of powdered sugar
- 1 tsp of vanilla extract
- 1/4 cup of unsalted butter, softened

INSTRUCTIONS:
1. Preheat the oven to 350°F (175°C). Grease and flour a 9-inch cake pan.
2. In a large bowl, mix together flour, sugar, baking soda, salt, cinnamon, and nutmeg.
3. In another bowl, whisk together sourdough discard, vegetable oil, and eggs until blended. Stir this into the dry ingredients until just combined.
4. Fold in the grated carrots.
5. Pour the batter into the prepared cake pan. Smooth the top with a spatula.
6. Bake for 35-40 minutes, or until a toothpick inserted into the center of the cake comes out clean.
7. While the cake is cooling, make the frosting. Beat together the cream cheese, powdered sugar, vanilla, and butter until smooth.
8. Once the cake has fully cooled, spread the frosting evenly over the top. Cut into pieces and serve. Enjoy your Sourdough Discard Carrot Cake!

CHERRY CLAFOUTIS

Preparation time: 15 minutes
Cooking time: 45 minutes
Servings: 4

INGREDIENTS:
- 1 cup of Sourdough Discard
- 2 cups of Fresh, pitted cherries
- 1 cup of Whole milk
- 3 Large eggs
- 1/2 cup of Granulated sugar
- 1 tablespoon of Vanilla extract
- 1/8 teaspoon of Salt
- Powdered sugar for dusting (Optional)

INSTRUCTIONS:
1. Preheat your oven to 375 degrees F (190 degrees C). Grease a 9-inch pie dish lightly with non-stick spray or butter.
2. Distribute the pitted cherries evenly across the bottom of the dish.
3. In a blender or food processor, add the sourdough discard, eggs, whole milk, granulated sugar, vanilla extract, and salt. Blend

until the mixture is smooth and well combined.

4. Pour the batter over the cherries in the pie dish, ensuring that all the cherries are covered.

5. Place the dish in the oven and bake for about 45 minutes. The clafoutis is done when it's puffed up and golden, and a knife inserted in the center comes out clean.

6. Allow the clafoutis to cool for a few minutes after taking it out of the oven. Note that it will deflate slightly.

7. Dust the top with powdered sugar if desired.

8. Serve your Sourdough Discard Cherry Clafoutis warm.

CHOCOLATE BABKA

Preparation time: 180 minutes
Cooking time: 45 minutes
Servings: 4

INGREDIENTS:
For the dough:
- 1 cup sourdough starter discard
- 3 cups all-purpose flour
- 1/4 cup granulated sugar
- 1/2 cup warm milk
- 1 large egg
- 1/2 cup unsalted butter, softened
- 1/4 teaspoon salt

For the filling:
- 1 1/2 cups semi-sweet chocolate chips
- 1/4 cup powdered sugar

- 1/2 teaspoon cinnamon
- 1/4 cup unsalted butter

For the syrup:
- 1/4 cup granulated sugar
- 1/4 cup water

INSTRUCTIONS:
1. Begin by combining the sourdough discard, flour, sugar, warm milk, egg, butter, and salt in a large mixing bowl. Knead until the dough is smooth and elastic.

2. Cover the dough and let rise in a warm place for about two hours, until it has doubled in size.

3. Meanwhile, prepare the chocolate filling. Melt the chocolate chips and butter together in a microwave or over a pot of simmering water. Stir in the powdered sugar and cinnamon until fully combined.

4. Once the dough has risen, punch it down and roll it out on a lightly floured surface into a rectangle about 1/2-inch thick.

5. Spread the chocolate filling evenly over the dough, leaving a border around the edges.

6. Roll the dough up tightly from one of the long sides, like a jelly roll. Slice the roll in half lengthways, and then twist the two halves together, cut sides facing up.

7. Place the dough in a buttered loaf pan, cover, and let rise for another hour.

8. Preheat the oven to 350°F. Bake the babka for about 45 minutes,

until it's golden brown on top and a skewer inserted into the middle comes out clean.

9. While the babka is baking, make the syrup by combining the sugar and water in a small saucepan over medium heat. Stir until the sugar has dissolved, then remove from heat.

10. As soon as the babka comes out of the oven, brush it generously with the syrup. Allow to cool in the pan for 10 minutes, then transfer to a wire rack to cool completely.

11. Enjoy this delicious Sourdough Discard Chocolate Babka as a decadent breakfast or dessert. The sourdough discard adds a unique tangy flavor that balances perfectly with the rich chocolate.

CHOCOLATE CAKE

Preparation time: 20 minutes
Cooking time: 35-40 minutes
Servings: 4

INGREDIENTS:
- 1 cup of sourdough discard
- 1 and 1/2 cups of all-purpose flour
- 1 cup of white granulated sugar
- 1/2 cup of unsweetened cocoa powder
- 1 teaspoon of baking soda
- 1/2 teaspoon of salt
- 1/2 cup of vegetable oil
- 1 cup of water
- 1 teaspoon of pure vanilla extract
- 1 tablespoon of white vinegar
- Powdered sugar for dusting (optional)

INSTRUCTIONS:
1. Preheat your oven to 350°F. Grease and flour an 8-inch round cake pan.
2. In a large bowl, combine the flour, sugar, cocoa powder, baking soda and salt. Mix well until all dry ingredients are thoroughly combined.
3. In a separate bowl, combine the sourdough discard, water, vegetable oil, and vanilla extract. Mix well to combine.
4. Gradually add the wet ingredients into the dry mixture, stirring continuously to ensure they are well combined.
5. Add the vinegar to the batter and fold briefly until it is evenly distributed throughout the batter.
6. Pour the batter to the prepared cake pan and distribute evenly.
7. Bake in the preheated oven for 35-40 minutes, or until a toothpick inserted into the center comes out clean.
8. Allow the cake to cool in the pan for about 10 minutes, and then transfer to a wire rack to cool completely.
9. Once cooled, dust the top of the cake with powdered sugar if desired. Slice and serve.

CHOCOLATE CHIP COOKIES

Preparation time: 20 minutes
Cooking time: 10 minutes
Servings: 4

INGREDIENTS:

- 1/2 cup of softened unsalted butter
- 1/4 cup of granulated sugar
- 1/2 cup of packed brown sugar
- 1 large egg
- 1/2 teaspoon of pure vanilla extract
- 1 cup of all-purpose flour
- 1/2 teaspoon baking soda
- 1/4 teaspoon of salt
- 1 cup of sourdough discard
- 1.5 cups of semisweet chocolate chips

INSTRUCTIONS:

1. Preheat your oven to 375°F (190°C) and line a baking sheet with parchment paper.
2. In a large bowl, cream together the softened butter, granulated sugar, and brown sugar until they're well combined and creamy.
3. Add the egg and vanilla extract to your butter and sugar mixture and mix until they're fully combined.
4. In another bowl, mix together the all-purpose flour, baking soda, and salt.
5. Gradually add the dry ingredients into the wet ingredients, stirring after each addition.
6. Once those are combined, fold in the sourdough discard until it's well combined with the rest of the dough.
7. Stir in the semisweet chocolate chips until they're evenly distributed throughout the cookie dough.
8. Drop your cookie dough onto the prepared baking sheet in 1.5 tablespoon portions, with about 2 inches of space between each cookie for spreading.
9. Bake the cookies in your preheated oven for 10-12 minutes, or until they're golden brown around the edges.
10. Remove your cookies from the oven and let them cool on the baking sheet for a few minutes, then transfer them to a wire rack to finish cooling.

CHOCOLATE TRUFFLES

Preparation time: 25 minutes
Cooking time: 2 hours
Servings: 4

INGREDIENTS:

- 4 ounces good quality Semisweet Chocolate
- 2 tablespoons Unsalted Butter
- 3 tablespoons Sourdough Discard
- 2 tablespoons Heavy Cream
- 1 tablespoon Dark Rum (optional)
- 1/4 cup Cocoa Powder, for rolling

INSTRUCTIONS:

1. Break the chocolate into small pieces and put it in a heatproof bowl along with the butter. Set the bowl over a pot of gently simmering water, ensuring the bowl doesn't touch the water. Stir occasionally until the chocolate and butter have melted and combined.
2. Remove the bowl from the heat and stir in the sourdough discard, heavy cream, and rum if using. Once well mixed, refrigerate the mixture for about 2 hours, or until it's firm enough to shape.
3. Scoop out small spoonsful of the truffle mixture and roll into balls. If the mixture is too sticky to handle, dust your hands with a little cocoa powder.
4. Roll the formed truffles in the cocoa powder to coat, then place them on a silicone mat or a piece of parchment paper.
5. Store your Sourdough Discard Chocolate Truffles in the refrigerator until you're ready to serve them. These indulgent treats will keep in the fridge for up to 2 weeks.

COCONUT MACAROONS

Preparation time: 15 minutes
Cooking time: 20 minutes
Servings: 4

INGREDIENTS:
- 1/2 cup of sourdough starter discard
- 2 cups of sweetened shredded coconut
- 1/2 cup of granulated white sugar
- 2 large egg whites
- 1 teaspoon of vanilla extract
- 1/4 teaspoon of salt

INSTRUCTIONS:
1. Preheat your oven to 325°F (165°C) and line a baking sheet with parchment paper.
2. In a mixing bowl, combine the sourdough starter discard, shredded coconut, sugar, egg whites, vanilla extract, and salt. Mix until everything is well incorporated.
3. Using a cookie scoop or tablespoons, scoop out the mixture and shape into small mounds. Place them on the prepared baking sheet, leaving some space between each macaroon as they will spread out slightly during baking.
4. Bake in the preheated oven for about 18-20 minutes, or until the edges and bottoms are golden brown. The tops of the macaroons should be lightly colored.
5. Remove from the oven and let them cool on the baking sheet for at least 10 minutes. Then move them to a wire rack to cool completely.
6. Enjoy your Sourdough Discard Coconut Macaroons as a tasty treat! It's a great way to reduce

waste and enjoy a delicious dessert.

DONUTS

Preparation time: 15 minutes
Cooking time: 30 minutes
Servings: 4

INGREDIENTS:
- 1 cup of sourdough discard
- 2 cups of all-purpose flour
- 1/2 cup of sugar
- 2 teaspoons of baking powder
- 1/2 teaspoon of baking soda
- 1/2 teaspoon of salt
- 3/4 cup of milk
- 2 large eggs
- 3 tablespoons of vegetable oil
- 1 teaspoon of vanilla extract
- Glaze of choice (optional)

INSTRUCTIONS:
1. Preheat your oven to 375°F and grease a donut pan.
2. In a large mixing bowl, combine flour, sugar, baking powder, baking soda, and salt.
3. In another bowl, whisk together the sourdough discard, milk, eggs, vegetable oil, and vanilla extract until well combined.
4. Gradually add the dry ingredients to the wet ingredients, stirring gently until just combined. Be careful not to overmix.
5. Fill each donut well 2/3 full of batter. You can use a piping bag or a spoon.

6. Bake for 12-15 minutes, or until the donuts spring back when lightly pressed.
7. Allow the donuts to cool in the pan for about 5 minutes, then remove them to a cooling rack.
8. When the donuts are cool enough to handle but still slightly warm, dip each one into your chosen glaze (if using), then return them to the cooling rack to allow the glaze to set.
9. Serve these light and airy Sourdough Discard Donuts with a cup of coffee or tea for a delicious treat.

GINGERBREAD COOKIES

Preparation time: 20 minutes
Cooking time: 10 minutes
Servings: 4

INGREDIENTS:
- 1/2 cup unsalted butter, softened
- 1/2 cup granulated sugar
- 1/2 cup sourdough discard, at room temperature
- 1/3 cup molasses
- 1 large egg
- 2 1/4 cups all-purpose flour
- 2 teaspoons ground ginger
- 1 teaspoon ground cinnamon
- 1/2 teaspoon ground cloves
- 1/2 teaspoon baking soda
- 1/4 teaspoon salt
- Additional granulated sugar, for rolling

INSTRUCTIONS:

1. Preheat your oven to 375°F (190°C) and line a baking sheet with parchment paper.
2. In a large bowl, cream together the butter and sugar until light and fluffy.
3. Add the sourdough discard, molasses, and egg to the butter mixture and beat until well combined.
4. In a separate bowl, whisk together the flour, ginger, cinnamon, cloves, baking soda, and salt.
5. Gradually add the dry ingredients to the wet mixture, mixing just until combined. The dough will be slightly sticky.
6. Using your hands, roll the dough into 1-inch balls. Roll each ball in granulated sugar to coat.
7. Place the balls onto the prepared baking sheet, spaced about 2 inches apart.
8. Bake for 10 minutes, or until the cookies are set around the edges and slightly cracked on top.
9. Allow the cookies to cool on the baking sheet for a few minutes, then transfer them to a wire rack to cool completely.
10. Enjoy your Sourdough Discard Gingerbread Cookies with a cup of hot tea or coffee!

LEMON BARS

Preparation time: 30 minutes
Cooking time: 40 minutes
Servings: 4

INGREDIENTS:
For the crust:
- 1 cup of sourdough discard
- 1/2 cup of unsalted butter, melted
- 1/4 cup of granulated sugar
- 1 cup of all-purpose flour
- Pinch of salt

For the lemon filling:
- 1 cup of granulated sugar
- 2 large eggs
- 2 tablespoons of all-purpose flour
- 1/4 cup of freshly squeezed lemon juice
- Zest of 1 fresh lemon
- Powdered sugar for dusting

INSTRUCTIONS:
1. Preheat your oven to 350 degrees F (175 degrees C) and line an 8x8 inch baking dish with parchment paper.
2. In a large mixing bowl, combine the sourdough discard, melted butter, sugar, flour, and salt to make the crust. Press the mixture firmly into the bottom of the lined baking dish.
3. Bake the crust in the preheated oven for around 15-20 minutes, or until it's lightly golden.
4. Meanwhile, prepare the lemon filling. In a separate bowl, whisk together the sugar and eggs until smooth. Add in the flour, lemon juice, and zest, continuing to whisk until the mixture is well combined.

5. Once the crust is done baking, reduce the oven temperature to 325 degrees F (163 degrees C). Pour the lemon filling over the hot crust and return it to the oven for 20-25 minutes, or until the filling is set.
6. Allow the lemon bars to completely cool before cutting into squares. Dust them generously with powdered sugar before serving.

MUG CAKE

Preparation time: 5 minutes
Cooking time: 1.5 minutes per mug
Servings: 4

INGREDIENTS:
- 1/2 cup of sourdough starter discard
- 4 tablespoons of unsalted butter
- 2/3 cup of sugar
- 1 cup of all-purpose flour
- 4 eggs
- 2 teaspoons of vanilla extract
- 4 teaspoons of baking powder
- 1/2 teaspoon of salt
- 2/3 cup of milk
- Optional: 4 tablespoons of chocolate chips or other preferred mix-ins

INSTRUCTIONS:
1. First, divide the butter between the four microwave-safe mugs. Melt it in the microwave for about 30 seconds or until it fully melts.

2. After the butter is melted, stir in the sugar until it is fully incorporated.
3. In a separate bowl, whisk together flour, baking powder, and salt.
4. Gradually add the flour mixture into the mugs, stirring after each addition.
5. Stir in the sourdough discard, vanilla extract, and eggs into each mug until you have a smooth batter. Make sure to mix well.
6. Next pour in the milk and stir until well combined.
7. Add your mix-ins (e.g., chocolate chips) if desired and mix them into the batter.
8. Place one mug at a time in the microwave and cook on high for 1.5 minutes. Be sure to monitor each mug cake because cooking times can vary depending on the wattage of your microwave. Cake should ""spring"" back to the touch when done and not look too wet.
9. Carefully remove the mug from the microwave (it will be hot), let it cool for a couple of minutes, and enjoy straight from the mug or turned out onto a plate.
10. Repeat microwave cooking with the remaining mugs.

OATMEAL COOKIES

Preparation time: 20 minutes
Cooking time: 15 minutes

Servings: 4

INGREDIENTS:

- 1 cup of sourdough discard
- 1 cup of all-purpose flour
- 1 cup of rolled oats
- 1/2 cup of unsalted butter, softened
- 1/2 cup of granulated sugar
- 1/2 cup of packed brown sugar
- 1 large egg
- 1/2 teaspoon of baking soda
- 1/2 teaspoon of salt
- 1/2 teaspoon of cinnamon
- 11/2 teaspoon of vanilla extract

INSTRUCTIONS:

1. Preheat the oven to 350°F (175°C) and line two baking sheets with parchment paper.
2. In a large bowl, combine the sourdough discard, all-purpose flour, and rolled oats.
3. In another bowl, beat together the softened butter, granulated sugar, and brown sugar until fluffy. Add the egg and vanilla extract, beating until well combined.
4. Gradually add the dry ingredients to the butter mixture and mix until well combined.
5. Stir-in the baking soda, salt, and cinnamon into the cookie dough.
6. Drop tablespoons of dough onto the prepared baking sheets, spacing them about 2 inches apart.
7. Bake in the preheated oven for 12-15 minutes, or until the edges are golden brown.
8. Allow the cookies to cool on the baking sheet for 10 minutes before moving them to a wire rack to cool completely.
9. Enjoy your Sourdough Discard Oatmeal Cookies as a delightful snack!

PEACH COBBLER

Preparation time: 20 minutes
Cooking time: 45 minutes
Servings: 4

INGREDIENTS:

- 1 cup of sourdough discard
- 1 1/2 cups all-purpose flour
- 1/4 cup granulated sugar
- 2 teaspoons baking powder
- 1/2 teaspoon salt
- 8 tablespoons unsalted butter
- 1/2 cup milk
- 3 cups of peeled and sliced fresh peaches
- 1/2 cup brown sugar
- 1 tablespoon cornstarch
- 1/4 teaspoon ground cinnamon
- 1/4 teaspoon ground nutmeg
- Juice of 1/2 lemon

INSTRUCTIONS:

1. Preheat your oven to 375°F (190°C). Grease a 9-inch baking dish and set it aside.
2. In a large bowl, combine fresh peaches, brown sugar, cornstarch, cinnamon, nutmeg,

and lemon juice. Toss gently until well combined and all peaches are coated in the sugar mixture.

3. Transfer the peach mixture to the prepared baking dish. Spread them out evenly.
4. In another bowl, combine all-purpose flour, granulated sugar, baking powder and salt. Add in the sourdough discard.
5. Melt the butter and add it to the flour mixture, along with the milk. Stir until just combined.
6. Drop spoonsful of the biscuit topping over the peaches in the baking dish. It is okay if some of the peaches are peeking through the topping.
7. Bake in the preheated oven for about 45 minutes, or until the topping is golden brown and the peaches are bubbly.
8. Allow the cobbler to cool for about 10 minutes before serving. This dish is best served warm, with a scoop of vanilla ice cream on top if desired.
9. Enjoy this delightful and tangy twist on peach cobbler made with the convenient and delicious use of sourdough discard.

PEANUT BUTTER COOKIES

Preparation time: 15 minutes
Cooking time: 10 minutes
Servings: 4

INGREDIENTS:
- 1 cup of Sourdough Discard
- 1/2 cup of Peanut Butter
- 1/2 cup of Granulated Sugar
- 1/4 cup of Brown Sugar
- 1/2 cup of Unsalted Butter, at room temperature
- 1 Large Egg
- 1/2 teaspoon of Vanilla Extract
- 1/2 teaspoon of Baking Soda
- 1/2 teaspoon of Baking Powder
- 1/4 teaspoon of Salt
- 1 3/4 cups of All-Purpose Flour
- 1/2 teaspoon of Ground Cinnamon (optional)

INSTRUCTIONS:
1. Preheat your oven to 375 degrees. Line two baking sheets with parchment paper or silicone baking mats.
2. In the bowl of a stand mixer equipped with a paddle attachment, cream together the butter, peanut butter and both sugars until light and fluffy.
3. Beat in the egg, followed by the vanilla and sourdough discard, mixing until well incorporated.
4. In a separate bowl, whisk together the flour, baking soda, baking powder, salt, and cinnamon (if using).
5. Gradually add the dry ingredients to the wet ingredients, mixing until just combined.
6. Use a cookie scoop or spoon to place dough onto prepared baking sheets, spacing cookies about 2 inches apart.
7. Flatten the tops of the cookies slightly with your fingers or the

back of a spoon. This will allow them to bake more evenly.

8. Bake for about 10 minutes until the edges are slightly golden. Let them cool on the baking sheets for a couple of minutes, then transfer to a wire rack to cool completely.

9. Enjoy these Sourdough Discard Peanut Butter Cookies with a glass of cold milk or your favorite hot beverage.

RASPBERRY BARS

Preparation time: 20 minutes
Cooking time: 55 minutes
Servings: 4

INGREDIENTS:
- 1 1/2 cups all-purpose flour
- 1 cup sugar, divided
- 1/2 teaspoon baking powder
- 1/2 teaspoon salt
- 1/2 cup unsalted butter, cold and cubed
- 1 cup sourdough starter discard
- 1 teaspoon cinnamon
- 2 cups fresh raspberries
- 1 tablespoon cornstarch
- 1 tablespoon lemon juice

INSTRUCTIONS:
1. Preheat your oven to 375°F and line an 8x8 inch baking dish with parchment paper.

2. In a food processor, pulse together the flour, half of the sugar, baking powder, salt, and cinnamon. Add the cold butter and pulse until coarse crumbs form.

3. Add the sourdough discard and pulse again until a dough forms.

4. Press two-thirds of the dough into the bottom of the prepared baking dish to form a crust. Set aside the other third for the topping.

5. Bake the crust in the preheated oven for 10 minutes, or until it starts to turn golden brown.

6. While the crust is baking, toss together the raspberries, the remaining sugar, cornstarch, and lemon juice in a medium bowl.

7. When the crust is ready, spread the raspberry mixture evenly over the top.

8. Crumble the remaining dough over the raspberry layer.

9. Return the dish to the oven and bake for an additional 45 minutes, or until the top is golden brown and the filling is bubbling.

10. Let the bars cool completely in the dish on a wire rack before removing and slicing into individual servings.

DOUGHS & BATTERS

BAO BUNS

Preparation time: 2 hours 30 minutes
(includes dough resting time)
Cooking time: 15 minutes
Servings: 4 people

INGREDIENTS:
- 1.5 cups of sourdough discard
- 1/2 cup of warm water
- 2 teaspoons of active dry yeast
- 1 tablespoon of sugar
- 3.5 cups of bread flour
- 1/2 teaspoon of table salt
- 1/4 cup of vegetable oil

INSTRUCTIONS:
1. In a large bowl, combine the warm water and sugar until the sugar is fully dissolved.
2. Sprinkle the active dry yeast over the water and allow it to activate for about 5-10 minutes. You'll know it's ready when it begins to froth.
3. To this yeast mixture, add the sourdough discard and mix well.
4. Gradually add in the bread flour and table salt.
5. Once a dough begins to form, slowly start adding the vegetable oil while continuously mixing.
6. Knead the dough either by hand or with a stand mixer for about 10 minutes or until it becomes smooth and stretchy.
7. Place the dough in a lightly oiled bowl, cover with a kitchen towel, and let it rest in a warm spot for about 2 hours. The dough should approximately double in size.
8. After the dough has rested, divide it into 16 equal portions.
9. Form each portion into a ball and flatten them gently with your palm to create the bun shape.
10. Place each bun on a piece of parchment paper and leave them to rest for an additional 30 minutes.
11. While the buns are resting, bring a pot of water to a boil and set up a steamer.
12. Once the water is boiling, arrange the buns in the steamer (make sure they are not touching), cover and steam for about 15 minutes.
13. Serve the buns warm as they are or filled with your choice of filling.

CHAPATI

Preparation time: 15 minutes
Cooking time: 15 minutes
Servings: 4

INGREDIENTS:
- 2 cups of all-purpose flour
- 1 cup of sourdough discard
- 1/2 cup of water (more or less may be needed)
- 1 tablespoon of vegetable oil
- 1 teaspoon of salt

INSTRUCTIONS:
1. In a large bowl, combine the flour and salt. Make a well in the middle and add the sourdough discard.

2. Bit by bit, add water and start to bring the ingredients together. Initially go for a shaggy dough.
3. Add the vegetable oil and continue to knead the dough. It should be soft and smooth. Knead for around 5 minutes.
4. Set the dough aside, covering it with a damp cloth. Leave it to rest for about 20-30 minutes.
5. Once the dough has rested, divide it into 8 equal parts. Using your hands, shape these into balls.
6. Dust a clean surface with flour. Take one dough ball and roll it into a thin, round chapati, about 6-7 inches in diameter.
7. Heat a pan on medium heat. Once hot, add the rolled dough. Cook for about 2 minutes on medium heat.
8. Flip the chapati when it starts to puff up and show little brown spots on it. Cook the other side too until you see similar brown spots.
9. Repeat the process with the rest of the dough balls.
10. You can add butter or ghee on top if desired. Serve the sourdough discard chapati warm with a curry of your choice.

NAAN

Preparation time: 90 minutes
Cooking time: 30 minutes
Servings: 4

INGREDIENTS:
- 1 cup of sourdough discard
- 2 1/2 cups of all-purpose flour
- 1/2 cup of whole milk
- 1 tablespoon of melted ghee or butter
- 1/2 teaspoon of baking powder
- 1/2 teaspoon of salt
- 1/4 cup of yogurt
- Optional: Minced garlic, cilantro, and extra ghee or butter for garnishing.

INSTRUCTIONS:
1. Combine the sourdough discard, all-purpose flour, milk, melted ghee, baking powder, salt, and yogurt in a large mixing bowl. Stir until a dough is formed.
2. Knead the dough on a floured surface until it is smooth and elastic, about 10 minutes.
3. Place the dough back in the bowl, cover with a clean kitchen towel and let it rest for about an hour.
4. After the dough has rested, divide it into 8 equal pieces. Roll each piece into a ball.
5. Heat a large skillet or griddle over medium heat. Flatten each dough ball with a rolling pin into a naan shape.
6. Cook each naan on the heated skillet, flipping once, until golden brown on both sides, about 2 minutes per side.
7. Optional: Brush with additional melted ghee and sprinkle with

minced garlic and cilantro for garnish.

8. Serve your sourdough discard naan hot, alongside your favorite Indian curries or dips. Enjoy

EMPANADA DOUGH

Preparation time: 15 minutes
Cooking time: 20 minutes
Servings: 4

INGREDIENTS:
- 1 cup of sourdough discard
- 2.5 cups of all-purpose flour
- 1 teaspoon of salt
- 1 teaspoon of baking powder
- 1/2 cup of unsalted butter, cold and cut into small pieces
- 3/4 cup of ice water

INSTRUCTIONS:
1. In a large mixing bowl, combine the sourdough discard, all-purpose flour, salt, and baking powder. Stir until well blended.
2. Add the cold, cubed butter to the flour mixture. Using your fingers, work the butter into the flour until it forms a crumbly texture.
3. Gradually add the ice water, stirring with a fork until a dough forms. You may not need the entire 3/4 cup, so add slowly and stop once the dough comes together.
4. Transfer the dough onto a lightly floured surface and knead until smooth.

5. Divide the dough into 4 equal balls, wrap each in plastic wrap and refrigerate for at least 1 hour before using. This allows the dough to rest and the butter to chill, which will result in a flakier empanada.
6. When ready to use, roll out each dough ball to about 1/8-inch thickness and cut into 4–6-inch rounds, depending on how large you want your empanadas to be.
7. Your Sourdough Discard Empanada Dough is now ready to be filled and cooked according to your favorite empanada recipe.

SKILLET BREAD

Preparation time: 15 minutes
Cooking time: 20 minutes
Servings: 4

INGREDIENTS:
- 2 cups of sourdough starter discard
- 1/4 cup of olive oil
- 1/4 cup of water
- 1 cup all-purpose flour
- 1 tsp baking powder
- 1/2 tsp baking soda
- 1/2 tsp salt
- 1/2 tsp garlic powder (optional)
- 2 tbsp chopped fresh herbs (optional)
- 1 cup of shredded cheddar cheese (optional)

INSTRUCTIONS:

1. Preheat your oven to 425°F (220°C). Drizzle olive oil in a 10-inch cast-iron skillet, spreading it up the sides with a paper towel. Place the skillet in the oven to heat up.
2. In a large bowl, combine the sourdough discard, water, and flour. Stir until the mixture is roughly combined.
3. In a smaller bowl, combine the baking powder, baking soda, salt, garlic powder (if using), and chopped herbs (if using). Sprinkle this mixture over the sourdough mixture but don't stir it in yet.
4. Take your hot skillet out of the oven carefully using oven gloves. Make sure it's evenly coated with olive oil.
5. Stir the dry ingredients into the sourdough mixture until thoroughly combined. If you're adding cheese, stir it in now. The mixture will be thick and slightly sticky.
6. Spoon the batter into the hot skillet. Using the back of a spoon, smooth it out to the edges.
7. Bake the bread in the preheated oven for 20 minutes, or until the top is nicely browned and a knife inserted into the middle comes out clean.
8. Remove the skillet from the oven and let it cool on a wire rack for a few minutes before slicing the bread.
9. Enjoy this sourdough discard skillet bread warm, with some butter or a nice cheese it's perfect for dipping!

SPECIALITY TREATS

CHEESE PUFFS

Preparation time: 25 minutes
Cooking time: 25 minutes
Servings: 4

INGREDIENTS:
- 1 cup sourdough discard (unfed)
- 1 cup all-purpose flour
- 1/2 cup unsalted butter
- 1 cup water
- 1/2 teaspoon salt
- 4 large eggs
- 1 cup shredded sharp cheddar cheese
- 1/2 teaspoon garlic powder (optional)
- 1/2 teaspoon onion powder (optional)

INSTRUCTIONS:
1. Preheat your oven to 425°F (220°C). Line a baking sheet with parchment paper.
2. Bring the water, butter, and salt to a rolling boil in a medium-sized saucepan.
3. Stir in the flour all at once, continue to stir and cook the mixture until it forms a ball that doesn't separate.
4. Remove the pan from the heat, and let the mixture cool for 5-10 minutes. It should be warm to the touch but not so hot it will cook the eggs.
5. Transfer the mixture to a mixing bowl and beat in the eggs one by one. Make sure each is fully incorporated before adding the next. The mixture should become smooth.
6. Mix in the sourdough discard, followed by the shredded cheddar cheese, garlic powder, and onion powder.
7. Drop the batter by heaping tablespoonfuls onto the prepared baking sheet.
8. Bake the puffs in the preheated oven for 20 25 minutes, or until they've puffed up and turned golden brown.
9. Remove the puffs from the oven and serve warm.

COFFEE CAKE

Preparation time: 20 minutes
Cooking time: 25 minutes
Servings: 4 people

INGREDIENTS:
For the Cake:
- 1 cup of sourdough discard (at room temperature)
- 1/2 cup of granulated sugar
- 1/4 cup of unsalted butter (melted)
- 1 large egg
- 1 teaspoon of vanilla extract
- 1 cup of all-purpose flour
- 1 teaspoon of baking powder
- 1/4 teaspoon of baking soda
- 1/4 teaspoon of salt

For the Streusel Topping:
- 1/3 cup of brown sugar
- 2 tablespoons of all-purpose flour
- 1/2 teaspoon of ground cinnamon

- 2 tablespoons of unsalted butter (melted)

INSTRUCTIONS:
1. Preheat your oven to 350°F (175°C). Grease an 8-inch square baking dish, set aside.
2. To make the cake, in a large bowl, whisk together the sourdough discard, granulated sugar, melted butter, egg, and vanilla extract until well combined.
3. In a separate bowl, combine the flour, baking powder, baking soda, and salt.
4. Gradually add the dry ingredients to the wet ingredients, mixing until just combined. Pour the batter into the prepared baking dish.
5. Prepare the streusel topping: In a small bowl, combine the brown sugar, flour, and cinnamon. Pour in the melted butter and mix together with a fork until crumbly.
6. Sprinkle the streusel topping evenly over the batter in the baking dish.
7. Bake in the preheated oven for about 25-30 minutes, or until a toothpick inserted in the center comes out clean.
8. Allow the cake to cool in the pan for about 15 minutes. Then, slice and serve as a delightful morning treat.

CORN FRITTERS

Preparation time: 15 minutes
Cooking time: 20 minutes
Servings: 4

INGREDIENTS:
- 1 cup sourdough discard
- 1 cup all-purpose flour
- 1 1/2 cups fresh corn kernels
- 1 large egg
- 1/4 cup whole milk
- 1 tablespoon sugar
- 1 teaspoon baking powder
- 1/2 teaspoon salt
- 1/4 teaspoon freshly ground black pepper
- 1/4 cup chopped fresh chives
- Vegetable oil for frying

INSTRUCTIONS:
1. In a large bowl, stir together the sourdough discard, flour, corn kernels, egg, milk, sugar, baking powder, salt, pepper, and chives until evenly combined.
2. Heat a large skillet over medium heat and pour in enough oil to cover the bottom of the skillet.
3. Using a spoon, drop the batter into the skillet by the tablespoonful. Fry until the fritters are golden brown and cooked through, about 3-4 minutes per side.
4. Using a slotted spoon, transfer the fritters to a paper towel-lined plate to drain excess oil.

5. Repeat with the remaining batter, adding more oil to the skillet as needed.
6. Serve the fritters warm, as a side dish or appetizer.

CRANBERRY ORANGE SCONES

Preparation time: 30 minutes
Cooking time: 25 minutes
Servings: 4

INGREDIENTS:
- 1 ¼ cups all-purpose flour
- ½ cup granulated sugar
- 2 teaspoons baking powder
- ¼ teaspoon baking soda
- ½ teaspoon salt
- ¼ cup unsalted butter, cold and cubed
- 2/3 cup sourdough discard
- 1/3 cup milk
- ¾ cup dried cranberries
- Zest of 1 large orange
- Additional sugar for sprinkling

For the Glaze:
- 1 cup powdered sugar
- 3-4 tablespoons orange juice

INSTRUCTIONS:
1. Preheat your oven to 425°F (220°C). Line a baking sheet with parchment paper.
2. In a large bowl, combine the flour, sugar, baking powder, baking soda, and salt. Stir until well mixed.
3. Add the cubed butter to the flour mixture and use your fingers to work it in until the mixture resembles coarse crumbs.
4. Stir in the sourdough discard and milk until just combined. Don't overmix!
5. Gently fold in the dried cranberries and orange zest.
6. Turn the dough onto a floured surface and knead gently a few times to bring it together. Flatten into a disk about 1 inch thick.
7. Use a round biscuit cutter to cut out the scones and place them on the prepared baking sheet.
8. Sprinkle the tops of the scones with additional sugar.
9. Bake for 20-25 minutes, or until the scones are golden brown.
10. While the scones are baking, prepare the glaze by combining the powdered sugar and orange juice in a small bowl.
11. Allow the scones to cool for a few minutes after removing them from the oven, then drizzle with the orange glaze.
12. Serve warm and enjoy these flaky, tart, and zesty scones as a breakfast treat or with afternoon tea.

GRANOLA

Preparation time: 15 minutes
Cooking time: 30 minutes
Servings: 4

INGREDIENTS:

- 3 cups rolled oats
- 1 cup sourdough discard
- 1/2 cup unsweetened shredded coconut
- 1/2 cup raw pumpkin seeds
- 1/2 cup raw sunflower seeds
- 1/2 cup chopped almonds
- 1/2 cup raw honey
- 1 teaspoon vanilla extract
- 1 teaspoon ground cinnamon
- 1/4 teaspoon salt

INSTRUCTIONS:

1. Preheat your oven to 325°F (163°C) and line a large baking sheet with parchment paper.
2. In a large bowl, combine your oats, shredded coconut, seeds, and chopped almonds.
3. In a separate bowl, combine the sourdough discard, honey, vanilla extract, cinnamon, and salt. Stir until smooth.
4. Pour the wet mixture into your bowl of dry ingredients. Mix until all of your oats and nuts are coated.
5. Spread your granola mixture evenly on your prepared baking sheet.
6. Bake for 15 minutes.
7. Stir the granola on the baking sheet and then bake for another 15 minutes, or until your granola is golden brown and crispy.
8. Remove the granola from the oven and allow it to cool completely on the baking sheet. This will help it to continue to crisp up.
9. Once cooled, break up the granola into pieces and store in an airtight container for up to a week.
10. Enjoy your Sourdough Discard Granola on its own, or with yogurt, milk, or as a topping for fresh fruit.

GREEK YOGURT FLATBREAD

Preparation time: 70 minutes
Cooking time: 16 minutes
Servings: 4

INGREDIENTS:
- 1 cup of sourdough discard
- 1 1/2 cups of all-purpose flour
- 2 tablespoons of olive oil
- 1/2 cup of Greek yogurt
- 1 teaspoon of baking powder
- 1/2 teaspoon of salt

INSTRUCTIONS:

1. Start by combining your sourdough discard, all-purpose flour, baking powder, and salt in a mixing bowl. Stir them together until they are well mixed.
2. Add your Greek yogurt to the bowl. Use your hands or a spoon to mix the ingredients together until you have a smooth, cohesive dough. If it's a little sticky, add a sprinkle of flour and knead it in.
3. Once you have a good dough consistency, cover your bowl with a cloth or a plastic wrap and let it rest for about 60 minutes. This

allows the dough to rise slightly for a lighter flatbread.

4. After your dough has rested, preheat your oven to 475 degrees Fahrenheit. If you have a baking stone or a cast iron skillet, place it in the oven to preheat as well. If you don't have either, you can use a regular baking sheet, but there's no need to preheat it.

5. Take your dough out of the bowl and separate it into 4 balls. Roll each ball out on a floured surface until it's about 1/4 inch thick.

6. Brush each rolled out piece of dough with a bit of olive oil.

7. If you're using a baking stone or skillet, carefully remove it from the oven (remember it's hot!) and place one of your pieces of dough on it. If you're using a baking sheet, just place your dough on the sheet.

8. Bake each piece of dough for about 4 minutes, or until it puffs up and becomes lightly browned. Flip your dough and bake for another 2 minutes.

9. Repeat this process with the rest of your dough pieces.

10. Serve your sourdough discard Greek yogurt flatbread immediately, while it's still warm. It makes a great side dish for soups, salads, or as a base for personal pizzas.

MY HEARTFELT THANK YOU

Thank you for joining me on this delightful journey through the world of sourdough discard. I hope you found inspiration and joy in each recipe and discovered new ways to bring delicious, nutritious meals to your family while minimizing waste. Remember, the kitchen is your playground—don't be afraid to experiment and put your unique spin on these recipes.

Keep baking, keep exploring, and keep nurturing your passion for creating wholesome food. Your efforts not only fill your home with warmth and love but also contribute to a more sustainable world. Happy baking and may your sourdough adventures be ever rewarding!

With gratitude and best wishes,
Emma Brooks

By the way, do not forget to grab your 3 free bonuses. Scan the QR code below!
1. Sourdough Starter Secrets: A Beginner's Guide to Baking Bliss
2. Sourdough Solutions: Swift Fixes for Sourdough Struggles
3. Seasonal Swaps: Savvy Substitutions for Every Season